AF333732

BELONGING

Also by James McNeish

Tavern in the Town
Fire Under the Ashes
Mackenzie
The Mackenzie Affair
The Glass Zoo
As for the Godwits
Larks in a Paradise (with Marti Friedlander)
Art of the Pacific (with Brian Brake)

Plays

The Rocking Cave
The Mouse Man
1895

BELONGING

by
James McNeish

Research by
James and Helen McNeish

Holt, Rinehart and Winston
New York

This book is for
DOUGLAS

Copyright © 1980 by James McNeish

All rights reserved, including the right to reproduce
this book or portions thereof in any form.
Published by Holt, Rinehart and Winston,
383 Madison Avenue, New York, New York 10017.
Published simultaneously in Canada by Holt,
Rinehart and Winston of Canada, Limited.

Library of Congress Cataloging in Publication Data
Main entry under title:

Belonging.
   1. Israel—Biography. 2. Israel—Emigration
and immigration—Biography. I. McNeish, James.
CT1919.P35B44   920'.05694   79-19050
ISBN 0-03-046796-9

FIRST EDITION

Designed by I. Mandelbaum

Printed in the United States of America
10 9 8 7 6 5 4 3 2 1

None of the characters in this book is fictitious and
every resemblance to actual people, living or dead, is
intended. All the people and places are real. All the
people live in Israel.

Contents

	Preface	*vii*
1	Albert Winn	1
2	Amos Avriel	10
3	Erika Lewin	23
4	Sylva Zalmanson	47
5	Ada Sereni	66
6	Yoram Krivine	77
7	Nurit Shiloh	90
8	Olivia Zetler	107
9	Yuval Aloni	119
10	David Karon	129
11	Oula el-Aziz	140
12	Robert Mimouni	154
13	Uzi Davidson	162
14	Pastor Bob Lindsay	169
15	Abba Kovner	177
	Postscript	*188*
	Acknowledgments	*190*
	Glossary	*192*

Preface

Varda Mor
Literary Agent
Tel Aviv

My dear Varda,

I have been thinking of what you said when I walked in and announced this book. You said, if you remember, that the title is impossible, and I agree with you, but only in that it cannot be translated into Hebrew. You were contrary in other ways, too. You said, "Don't say I am beautiful or I'll call you a liar." Being Israeli, my dear, you would say that to any non-Jew who looked at you, and in any case I don't say it. I only say that you—like Israel—are a strange child among nations, quite unlike your parents, but I begin to see why you make others feel uncomfortable.

When you asked why I, a goy, should come so far to write about you, I said, "Because in New Zealand I have a fair chance to die in a bed." That threw you. But as you see, I haven't written only about you—there are Arabs and Christians here also. You were being presumptuous. As it happens, the title isn't mine; at least fifty people gave it to me. One said, "I was so lucky to be at home in the last war." That didn't throw me, but it threw my wife. My wife is from Czechoslovakia and where she comes from people say the opposite.

Yair said, "The sense of belonging starts the moment you get on the plane." Then I remembered. You don't know this but I came to Israel twice, both times with El Al. The first time, as the plane landed, everyone clapped their hands, the second time they burst into song. Something else you don't know is that before me my son came, though admittedly by mistake. He was seventeen. He spent three months on a kibbutz and to our horror grew up about three years. Now you may conclude from this that since I joined the human race I have been in a state of ignorance about your land and that my son's mistake gave me an excuse to repair it. It is as good a reason for this book as any.

Now listen, I have ignored all your advice, including your stern warning to avoid the topic of war (there is, I'm afraid, an episode on that). But please take comfort from the subject of the final chapter. Here I ignored the Foreign Office as well. They told me the subject was dead.

By the way, almost nobody wished to be anonymous, not even Uzi who returned from Entebbe. So except in two or three cases I have used real names.

Varda, I will be frank with you. Yours is the only country I know where in wartime people say, "I'm so lucky to be here," and in peace, "I wish to God I wasn't," then refuse to leave just for the pleasure of staying and making life impossible for one another. And then— this to a perfect stranger—throw up their hands and say, "Why is it?"

Jerusalem/London, 1977–79

Strangely enough, I like the kind to which I belong.

—The clown, in *The Clown*
(Heinrich Böll)

BELONGING

1

Albert Winn

I had just arrived in London and was standing on a street corner, when all of a sudden somebody said, "Hey, there's a war in Israel." Wow, I thought, that really messes up my plans. I was on my way to Europe and then Egypt before returning to the States. This guy on the street said, "I think there's a plane going out." I don't know how he knew.

I called the Israeli Embassy in London and I got right through. I said I'd heard there was a plane leaving for Israel and that my presence on it was vital. "Are you a doctor?" the voice said. Oh no, I thought, I should have become a doctor like my father. "No, but I can pick bananas." There was this silence at the other end. Then, "Don't be funny, there's a war going on." I thought the phone would be hung up on me.

"Look," I said, "this is the beginning of the banana-picking season. It's heavy work and only young people can do it. If there's a war going on, all the young people will be called away, and those bananas have to be picked. It's vital for the economy of the country. And I'm an *expert*."

So I was switched to somebody else who made me repeat the whole story. Then I was told, so casually I couldn't believe it, "There's a plane leaving in the morning. Be at the airport at seven o'clock."

I was there way before seven. I was the first in line, luckily, because the word had spread, and an hour later the place was mobbed like all get-out with Israelis, all pushing and shoving. The plane didn't leave until ten o'clock that night, but I didn't care. I had that ticket in my hand and that was all that mattered to me.

So that's what brought me back to Israel. I've just stayed here. I mean, it feels like this is my place, although sometimes when I look in the mirror I'm not too sure. My skin's changed color? My hair is different? Am I in the East or the West? Sometimes I think I can never fit into this place—it is *one great big collection of lunatics*. But maybe I feel more comfortable with lunatics. Especially Jewish lunatics.

It was a long war—three weeks. In Israel that is a long war. Except for reasons of health, everyone was involved or was close to someone who was involved in the fighting. Many of the kids on the plane with me went to fight straight from the airport.

After the war I decided I would try and live here. I remember going back to the States to talk with my parents about their Jewishness and mine, trying to find out where we were all at. I was never really sure, since in college I didn't get along with the Jewish kids. I was considered too Waspy. Then I was invited to join one of the non-Jewish fraternities, but I couldn't seem to find my place there either. "Dad," I said, "I've found something in Israel and I don't want to lose hold of it."

I stayed on the kibbutz through the war until the cease-fire, then went south to a center in Arad to learn Hebrew. It was full of immigrants. I was the Arad success story. The center had a full program in Hebrew and not only did I finish the course, but I stayed on and ended up assistant director.

Even then I wasn't sure. I used to sit in the dining room at Arad and watch the Russian immigrants pouring through and wonder what it was all about. There was one mother who would grab her kid by the back of the neck and whummp, stuff in the bread. Whummp, stuff in the potatoes. In five months I watched that Russian kid grow to enormous proportions. "Albert," I would say to myself, "you are supposed to have some *connection* with these people?"

It was my job to take upper-class American Jewish kids on trips around Israel to promote *aliya*, the great immigration. They would complain about the price of a falafel, about Israeli drivers, about the sand blowing. These were kids in their twenties, kids who had graduated from college.

One summer, her first day in the center, a girl came to me to say that she had spilled kerosene from the heater (from the heater!) all over the floor. Her husband had thrown a blanket over it. "Albert," she said, "would you send someone to the room to clean it up?" I said, "I hope you don't smoke." I mean with morons like her in this country who needs terrorists? I sent her back to the room and told her to push the doorbell, that someone would come. She pushed the doorbell and her husband came. Even then she didn't understand.

"They're not going to make it," I said to myself. And most of these American and English kids didn't. They gave up and went home.

I decided I had to get my hands dirty and come down into the desert, where I am now. It's not an oasis, it's just sand and rock. It's a long way from a big house in Philadelphia.

My father is a doctor, now retired and living in Florida. I grew up in Philadelphia, in a Jewish but not Zionist family. My two brothers are both doctors. One is a neurosurgeon at the University of Virginia and the other is an ophthalmologist in Florida.

I went to a small private boys' school. A select, Episcopalian school on the Main Line, which claimed to be nondenominational. A couple of blocks away was the Marion Cricket Club, a place where Jews are not welcome. I don't have a Jewish name and I don't look Jewish, so I went there anyway. My girlfriends were all non-Jewish.

I hated the draft and I certainly didn't intend to go to Vietnam. I remember the Penn State riots. I was there, but I kept well away from any of the violence. Then, when I was twenty-one, I came to Europe. I was just prancing around when I got to Munich. Next thing I'm at Dachau. They haven't even changed the name. Here I am, twenty-one, pop-eyed, standing in Dachau, and it's so spanking *clean*. And I thought, "Come on folks, it didn't look like this thirty years ago." It was the first time I felt that what happened may actually have happened. Because I was scared. I walked in and saw that crematorium and I was scared.

Suddenly, without thinking, I was on a plane flying to Israel for the first time. And here they were, Jews. They were all over the place. And not just some smelly old man in some awful synagogue mouthing out horrible old prayers in Hebrew, it was people. Wow, on Dizengoff on a Saturday night, walking down Dizengoff, and they are going crazy in Hebrew! They're eating ice cream in Hebrew, they're drinking Turkish coffee in Hebrew, making love in Hebrew—doing all kinds of things in Hebrew. I thought that was real keen.

One day last year I came down here and saw this settlement, this hill. This was after I told myself I had to roll up my sleeves and get my hands dirty. I had met some American kids coming to settle here, and I thought I'd visit for the weekend. "Why not stay a bit longer?" they said. They were just fifty families, and everyone was sort of struggling.

I came six months ago and I'm still here.

We're on a hill, exposed, in the middle of the desert. We're on a border, far from everything. The temperatures go up to 105°, 110°F. The sand blows around, it's on everything you touch.

We look out on a Jordanian police station and a military barracks. We're separated only by sand dunes. Where I work in the date fields that range of hills in Jordan is very close—on a clear day you can reach out and touch them. It's kind of scary. A few years ago there was a terrorist attack.

You've seen our watchtowers. To get in at night you

have to announce who you are. We have three soldiers stationed here, reservists. Every night the Israeli patrols come through. The Jordanians patrol the other side of the fence. The border is thirty yards away.

I haven't done my turn on guard duty yet. First I have to get some gun training. There's supposed to be a gun for every ten people.

I'll be thirty in August and I must be one of the oldest people here. All the Israelis are under thirty, although there's one elderly couple visiting. It's nice to see an old gray head here. There's a security in generations.

Who are my friends here? I have a lot of friends in Israel, many more than in the States. I was just thinking about that today, feeling lonely, I guess. But feeling lonely on the kibbutz, not in Israel. In America I also felt very lonely. Most of my friends here are American, and my closest friends are not Jewish but a Christian family living in Arad, who are also from Pennsylvania. They are *my family*.

Sometimes I get depressed. When I'm unhappy I get moody and start looking for a way out. My first week here I broke down completely. I walked into my room, closed the door, and was ready to cry. "What have I done to myself?" I said. In Arad everyone knew me. A letter would come marked "Albert—Arad," and it would find me. Here, all of a sudden I was running round with cows at four o'clock in the morning. It seemed like I was doing more working than breathing. And I hate cows.

The hardest thing here is getting adjusted. I'm still getting adjusted. After work I usually go to the pool and swim laps, then come back to my room and take a nap —that's about it. Once in awhile I'll stop and look at these four walls and realize I'm a long way from a big house in Philadelphia. If I was there now I could sneak off to the Seven-Eleven store on the corner and get myself a Canada Dry.

I don't say I haven't thought about going back. It has crossed my mind, but for what—to make my fortune selling display ads? If you believe that this place should exist, that it should be a living, breathing place, you should know it can't survive unless there are people living here. It's that simple. I mean, this country can't exist as some sort of Jewish Disneyland where people can send their money and have their names put on a building and then come and visit. Maybe I've got the people in the States all wrong, but being Jewish to them doesn't mean having an identity with Israel, it means belonging to a Jewish country club.

I don't miss the material things, but if you were to come to my room you'd understand why. I've got everything there. Okay, so I didn't get off a steerage boat with a pack on my back. As a matter of fact, I came on the Queen Elizabeth II—with five trunks of clothes, ten boxes of books, a record player, stuff from my father's place, some nice hand-turned chairs, and a Sheraton desk. But I've come. And *I'm* the one who speaks the language with "the funny accent." And I also dress funny and have an American mustache, not an Israeli beard. I'm a foreigner.

But I'm also an *oleh chadash*, a new immigrant—which is supposed to be a terrific *mitzvah*, a bonus. It means you've *ascended*. Well that's fine and dandy, until the whitewash wears off. You're still an immigrant.

By and large I've found Israelis to be fairly closed. I

sometimes wonder if they aren't even hostile toward some of us who've come. Maybe hostile is the wrong word, maybe just suspicious. "You come from America? You've had it good. What are you *doing* here?" It makes you wonder: Am I really wanted here? Is this the place for me? The people here don't know much about me. No one ever says, "Hey Albert, what makes you tick?" They don't ask questions. No one says, "Come on over, have a talk," yet it's implied that you're always welcome. Even at times when my Hebrew is at its best I find myself looking for some other American to talk to, someone who has some Western experiences to share. We used to do this a lot after work when the war was on, getting together just for the sake of being together.

Just loneliness, I guess.

This is a small kibbutz. In five minutes you can walk round the whole place. Today we finished planting the last of 238 date palms. Some of them weigh several hundred pounds. In the fall we'll begin picking the first date crop from trees that are five years old. We're already exporting chrysanthemums to Holland. I sort of feel like the dates are *my* dates. That's another reason for being here, because I'm in at the beginning—well, the almost-beginning.

This summer I'll be thirty and my temporary residency will run out, so if I decide to stay I will become an Israeli citizen. *If* I stay?

That's just it. I'm getting more into things. As time goes on I believe that if I work well, work hard, my name will spread. People will know me to be good. That's what gets you accepted around here—work. That doesn't bother me, what does is that everyone is so self-controlled, so *very* self-controlled. You keep wanting to walk up to people and shake them and say, "For crying out loud. Will someone show some *emotion*!"

I still receive the *Alumni News* from my prep school, and I get a *big* chuckle out of seeing "Kibbutz Grofit" on the address label. Under my Class Notes it says, "Albert Winn writes that he is living on a kibbutz." I just wonder what some of these people back there are thinking.

2
Amos Avriel

When I told my mother that I was going to a kibbutz, she said I was throwing my life away. She thought it was childish for anyone to place his trust in people—"You think people are *good*, Amos?" She thought they would cheat me, like in a business. They tell the joke about the fellow who went into a kibbutz and then wrote to his father, "I have so many cows and so many chickens and so much land." And his father wrote back, "I am happy, my son, that you are doing well and have so much property. But get rid of your partners."

I had this dream and it became a goal: life itself. I was already part of a nucleus that was connected with a kibbutz before we left Canada, an organization that believed not only that Palestine was a homeland but that you had to go there yourself and do something about it. People were building a new country, not only on the kibbutz but on the kibbutz *more so*—because there was no exploitation and people were cooperating more.

"Mother," I said, "the kibbutz makes for the greatest amount of security. You're making the whole community secure."

"You think it's a paradise, Amos?"

"Not only that," I said. "You can be secure and your conscience is at rest." I remember that at one time when I was going to work as a salesman for a fellow in Chicago and he wanted to impress me with the work I'd be doing, he said, "You have to be prepared to take the bread out of the next man's mouth." Which was putting it very aptly. I was there to get the business and to hell with Mr. Green. The more the hell with Mr. Green, the more successful I was. Oh, I did it. I wasn't a bad salesman, but it upset my stomach.

Anyway, my mother thought that coming to a kibbutz was abnormal. I was the only one from the whole neighborhood that came. I was like an idiot. For me, it was either going off to Palestine or going off to an insane asylum.

I was on the last ship that came before the war—actually during the war, 1940. The next group didn't make it. When I left Montreal my parents were so angry they said they'd have nothing to do with me. Later, when I wrote saying I was doing fine, they sent me a check. I sent it back. What did I want with money? What did money have to do with a better life? We were in it, we were doing it. We were living a life of values. We were living in between four drab gray walls, but we were sharing everything.

Everywhere I went I was writing poetry, except at work, and then, too, in my head. Work was something consecrated. When we picked stones from the field, that in itself was a total achievement. We worked for the sake of working. And it wasn't a question of working or not working, it was a question of working well, working more quickly, working to keep up with the Poles. The Poles were sovereign—they were the reigning group. They looked down on us and they were impatient because we couldn't keep up.

I was digging foundations. In the winter, every time you put one foot in the mud you never knew if it would come up with the shoe or without the shoe. We didn't have paths or anything. Later we worked with the *turea*, the big hoe, a murderous tool. It sounded romantic, but you spend ten minutes with that tool, all the romance goes out of it. In Canada I'd heard a Yiddish writer talking about kibbutz: "Oh, a group of romanticists sit at night and they watch the moon." Big deal.

In the kitchen they serve you half an egg, and you say to the one that's serving, "Maybe a little more? Another crumb?" That was all the egg we had for a whole week. Bean soup and a piece of margarine as big as my little finger. My teeth were transparent because we didn't have enough white cheese. We didn't have enough of anything. After I had typhus I was as thin as a rake, and as a special treat, I was given a small, very thin slice of sausage. We really weren't living it up.

I hadn't done a day's work in my life before I came. We were some fifty people surrounded by a sea of Arabs. Fifty of us, thirty thousand of them. Any minute, I thought, they are going to walk over us. How long can we live this way? Think, I'd say to myself. Think why you came, Amos.

I had malaria and typhoid fever at the same time, and I thought for sure I was going to die. They put me in the English government hospital, and I thought, This is the end, because the nurse came round and she said, "Doctor, look at his graph. *Look* at it. Here it goes up and here it goes down, here it looks like malaria, here it looks like typhus." He said, "But, my dear, he has both." They didn't know I spoke English and when he said "he has both," like that, so cheerfully, I thought that's it, I'm dead, because there were people round me dying of just one. But you pulled through and it didn't matter, none of this mattered—not the work you weren't used to, not the sun beating down, not the white cheese you craved or the hot water to shave in and the little conveniences you didn't have, not the Poles who didn't like you, because we all had one thing in common: we were building a new land. We were producing our own bread and we were no longer parasites. In God's eyes we were no longer parasites.

Privacy? We were living with six people in one room with no partitions. You could sit on your bed and read your own book by lamplight, if you could concentrate. Being alone? But this is no question for that time, because these were great times. Either you were broken or you had a great dream. And this dream was all-embracing, it was way above books and having your own little corner. It was divine, as I think of it now. And I think of it in connection with a time ten years later after I'd come back from prison and we were living in this little room. I looked outside and I said, "God Almighty, it can't be true. Only yesterday this was completely *nothing*, absolutely nothing. Can it be possible that all this came up because of these crazy people here?"

I saw houses—not glamorous buildings but real houses. I saw trees, blades of grass, a flower, children. I remember writing something about bringing a wrinkle to the Good Lord's brow. I wrote about God hovering over this place. It brought a wrinkle to His brow, which meant He was impressed.

Now, when I relate that to looking out of the window, it was as if we had lived there since the beginning of time. It was a dream come true, a living dream.

They tell a story about the Zionist who came to Israel for the first time and saw that Jews were really working the land by themselves. He turned to his friends: "You know all the lies I was preaching? I find they're really true." Well, at that moment when I looked out of the window, all those lies I'd been preaching *I* really believed in.

In prison I met many members of the Stern Gang—they were considered dangerous, and they were. They believed in personal reprisals, in killing the English wherever they could find them. I used to meet them walking in the yard and they would laugh at me.

I had been sentenced to twelve years for smuggling arms onto the kibbutz. When I came I was given a few days training on how to use a rifle, but we had no ammunition, practically nothing to shoot with, and I used to go on watch with these Italian rifles. There were eleven rifles to go round. They didn't shoot straight. They were terrible. If you put a few wisps of straw in the end you could use them as brooms.

Two of us volunteered for the Palmach. We arranged for a British army driver, a Jewish soldier, to bring in ammunition. I guess he split. We were caught red-handed. Big deal, I mean, there's not much heroism in being caught. After we were sentenced, I remember

I wrote to my friends in Canada and said, "Why me? I don't know what I have done to deserve this honor."

But we knew the kibbutz was behind us—the whole country was behind us. We had letters smuggled into prison telling us how the kibbutz was growing, how many chickens were being born, how many cows we had. . . . And here were these Stern people. They would sit and laugh at us for occupying our lives with such trivial things.

They believed that this was our land, rightfully ours. "What right?" I'd say. "By what right? Just because it's Jewish." Baloney. I didn't like their philosophy. *I* believed that we had to conquer the land by the sweat of our brow. I think a man has a right to any territory anywhere in the world that he desires to work with his own ten fingers. They couldn't understand this. They were good people—I mean they were dependable. I respected their dedication. But they could have been Nazis —the Nazis were dedicated too.

In prison I would just walk around in the yard all the time, but then something happened and I was told to work on the printing press. I refused. I wasn't going to work for the English and certainly not on their press, printing a magazine for the English police. Now the kibbutzniks got angry with me. They said I was betraying the cause of work. We had this song, *"Haavoda hi khayenu!"* ("Work Is Our Life")—it was sung all over the country. Work was holy; it was as if to work is to pray. I told them, "But you have to know *why* you're working." We had all come to Israel with the same ideals, but they seemed to have lost track of what they were doing. It sort of upset me.

What was our aim? The aim on kibbutz was a better life for human beings. We've gotten ahead in so many fields, we've even gotten to the moon, but people are still unhappy. Society does not seem to improve. So if I can make some dent, even a small dent, I've done a great thing. I wanted to build some society which would enable people to cooperate more.

Before I came, I had a very rosy picture of what kibbutz was like. I thought people would gang around me —"Come, brother Amos. Are you hungry, are you sleepy, are you tired? You need a clean pair of pajamas?" Well, nobody looked at you, nobody cared. Some things about kibbutz were nice, like sharing—we were doing that. But some things were not so nice.

I remember when I first got off the boat in Tel Aviv harbor and heard these hefty guys on the docks talking Hebrew. I was devastated. In Canada you never saw Jews in dirty clothes. When I was about eight, I once went with my mother to buy a pair of overalls. The woman in the shop said, "What do you want to be when you are big?" I said, "I want to be a worker." She said, "God forbid." And here were all these Godforbidden people on the docks hollering in Hebrew—I tell you it was like coming home after two thousand years.

But then we were walking along the street and we came to a flower seller. It was flower day. The man who had come to meet me at the boat just walked on. He said to the woman selling flowers, "I'm from a kibbutz," meaning he didn't have to buy a flower. I thought a man should have his own initiative.

And it was the same thing in prison when they ridiculed me for refusing to work. "Work for work's sake," they said. "Out of the habit comes the must." That was another slogan we repeated. But they weren't *thinking*.

After prison I went into grain growing in the fields. After prison, sitting on a tractor was a picnic. But some people were a bit sore. Because I wanted better housing, they said, "You want better housing? You *had* housing." They were a bit sore because I'd had this long rest in prison. I'd been in a building. They were living in tents.

We were taken from the prison in a car. I looked out of the window and I saw the hills. They looked like they were from a movie, they weren't real. If I'd walked up to them I couldn't have touched them. And I thought, How did the hills look before? And, Are they always going to look like that?

The view from the window doesn't improve. The people here are not particularly happy, no more than I am. Man's condition everywhere, I was thinking as I went out to work this morning, is to be basically unhappy.

I said to Moshe, this guy I work with, "Shalom. How are you?" He says, "*Yihyeh tov*. Things will be okay." He always says that, everyone says that. I don't know what people said a million years ago but if there's one thing I know they did say it's *yihyeh tov*. I remember this man in Canada. At one time he'd been a member of the movement. He was very unhappy because there was a club that only accepted people who had at least five million dollars, and he had only three million. He felt like a pauper. When you talked with him you felt you were talking to a very poor man.

When people in Canada said to me, "You think you

are going to a paradise?" I knew I couldn't stand my ground, so I looked for a way out and I said, "I'm going to a place that bears the least of evils." Just how few evils there were in this least of evils I didn't know. But I was convincing myself day to day that this is the right way.

We have done everything right. We have built the kibbutz. We are secure. I have enough. Everyone is equal, absolutely equal. But people don't just wake up in the morning and say, "Oh, brave new day. Today I'm going to share everything." People are not like that. I wish I could be like the wonderful people in *Exodus*, but I'm not. The people in that book are angels, not people.

Some people talk of the beginnings of this kibbutz when everything was "so ideal." It's *not* true. I remember lying on my bed one evening. Some people were talking outside of my door. They had been to the theater, which means they had their own money, which to my mind was illegal. On kibbutz you don't have your own money. They were talking quite openly about their sins. I was disappointed.

Dan Talmer came to the kibbutz a few years ago from Canada. He had a good business, a home of his own, three cars. He gave it all up. The other day, an old-timer asked me, "Why has this man Talmer come to the kibbutz?" I said to the old-timer, "Dan thinks the kibbutz is a better way of living." The old-timer, one of the founders, says, "Well, *is* it a better way of living?" I was very disappointed in him.

Now we have become affluent. They're giving out color television sets. Everyone has it coming to him as a right, whether he wants it or not. Does it make him any happier?

My little daughter Rachel was four when I took her to

Canada in 1960. All the time we were there she was longing for the kibbutz, and when we came back we found they had given us a new house. It had been built while we were away. We had been living in a wooden hut when we left. Rachel took one look at the house and burst into tears. She said, "It's not kibbutz any more."

The tragedy of kibbutz is that it doesn't grow. We haven't grown as we should. People don't flock to us. The rest of the world doesn't understand us. Sometimes I think our own children don't understand us. Do they say, "Abba, we're going to roll up our sleeves and finish what our parents haven't done?" Certainly not. They look on us with disdain that we don't live up to the standards we have set for ourselves. There's something in it. I've even heard children suggest "our parents brought us here as a sacrifice"—to die, like the symbol of Abraham offering his son Isaac as a sacrifice. "If you'd asked our opinion, how do you know we would have agreed to come?" This is the most dangerous place on earth.

Most of our kids are far superior to their parents as human beings. They share more easily than we do—my son to a fault. Yoel's door is always open, you can take anything. He'll give you his last pair of trousers. It's a wonderful thing. But see—our sons look down on us because we don't measure up to our ideals. So I say to Yoel, "But look at what we've got. We've got our homeland." Yoel says, "So what."

For him it's the most natural thing in the world. It's as if we'd had it forever. We had this dream of a better society. They just grew up here.

They say we have compromised. I agree, but only with religion. See, we have no religion. I wish I could be religious, but where I fall down is I don't believe. All the time I keep looking for this spiritual lift, and I don't get it. In Canada, in my parents' house, I could never understand why the light was brighter on the Sabbath. It's called the "extra soul." Each person has an extra or enlarged soul. It's true: the same soup you have in the weekday, on the Sabbath it tastes better. The house is brighter. The people look brighter. It's something we left behind. You know that until a year ago on Yom Kippur, the holiest day of the year, we worked? We were smart, but we weren't that smart. In the end we had to compromise. Practically all our traditions are steeped in the Jewish religion, and in the end we couldn't do without some sanctity.

You see, a horse doesn't know any better. But a human being needs a little lift in his life. So what do *we* do? Well, on the Sabbath you put a tablecloth on the table, a clean tablecloth. Somebody bakes a cake, and we look forward to the evening meal together—to which my son doesn't go.

I think where we went wrong is that we tried to bite off more than we could chew. We wanted to be very sharing people instead of very greedy people. Do you know that when we first came we had everything, but everything, in common—you didn't have your own pair of pants. You went to the commune and you took the pair of pants that was on top of the pile. Later, after someone had a real big brain wave, they gave them out according to sizes. Before, you could be a big guy and get a little pair of pants or a little guy and get a pair of pants you couldn't walk in because you tripped all over yourself. When the first new houses were built, we couldn't decide who was to live in them. So we drew lots and lived in them by turns. We had a goal and we were sharing everything to bring about that goal. But we weren't being very realistic.

People here are no different from people anywhere else. That we are God's Own People, I don't believe. People here are mean, are selfish, are exploiting, are greedy, are materialistic—like the people I left behind on the streets of Montreal, the same people. People don't live according to logic, they live according to their instincts and feelings, even here, where they are sharing and doing all the right things.

The difference is that here you share because you have to, because there is no alternative. What guards the kibbutz is the framework, not the people. For all these years I have been convincing myself that this is the right way —the least of evils. I still believe that. These weaknesses in people only prove it all the more.

All over the world people are preaching the life of kibbutz, but they don't want it for themselves because they don't like it. The kibbutzniks themselves don't like it because, as my mother said, it's "not natural." "So it's not natural," I say. "*That's* the reason there should be kibbutzim." Don't get me wrong—other people dream of villas or an extra automobile, we of a little more living space or just a little extra mileage for the kibbutz vehicle. Relatively speaking, we still share more than any other society I know. We may think like millionaires, but we still live like kibbutzniks.

I don't think the kibbutz will last forever. A long time ago I might have thought that more and more kibbutzim would grow up, that people would see it as a better thing. So why can't I be happy? The many setbacks here are to be expected, but they shock you anyway. I'm weak, I'm human, and I don't have the strength to withstand all the setbacks. Very few people have the strength.

How long can a dream last?

I'm staying. I'm here for ever and ever. I would live only in Israel—this is my castle. As a Jew this is my castle. I feel more sheltered here than anywhere else in the world. When I took my son Yoel to Canada, he said, "I want to see two things, a drunk and a Jew." He was twelve years old and he didn't know what a Jew was. That was a wonderful thing to say, I thought, and in Canada I told people this. Not that I ever suffered bad anti-Semitism myself in Canada; I didn't. It wasn't bad. But when I talked about anti-Semitism and told people they were being discriminated against, they were indignant. They were very angry I should suggest that such a thing existed.

It doesn't have to be extreme, it doesn't have to be a gas chamber. It can be a glance. I would say even to the extent where it lives in my imagination, that's enough.

Of course I may be wrong, I've been wrong before. Maybe everybody loves me.

3

Erika Lewin

When the Russian soldiers came they were all very sweet, very kind. Such beautiful smiles, such beautiful teeth. We were so excited, especially the young people. The young people welcomed them with flowers. They were so charming—"Little dove. Little bird. Little aunt. Little mother. . . . " They also shot you like that. "Little dove. Little bird. . . . "

We were lucky. My mother had been to a Ukrainian school so she spoke Russian and acted as interpreter. My father had a shop, a quarter share in a porcelain and glass shop. Every night the Russians came and asked us questions: about our past, about our relatives, family overseas. That was very important, family overseas. And then: "Where overseas?" It was all written down and the next week they came and asked us again. In the end we made jokes about the night hearings. A friend of mine said he was a doctor. And then they said, "Can you read or write?" They wanted to know whether he could read or write!

The Russians came into Rumania on June 28, 1940. Nothing happened for almost a year, and then one night they took us. Ten days after they took us, the Nazis came. It was only ten days; really, the Russians saved us from the Nazis, only most of us died anyway.

We were not frightened, just puzzled and confused. What had we done? I had been ill with tuberculosis for two years. I was giving piano lessons. I wanted to be a pianist. My husband was a clerk. He was at one time an active Communist—he had even been imprisoned for being a Communist—but that didn't seem to help. "It must have been for hooliganism," they said. The Russians didn't believe you could be a Communist voluntarily.

We had exchanged our bad passports for good ones. We were not active politically, everything was all right. I was looking after my sick grandfather—he fortunately died before that night. And then without a hearing, without any hearing at all, there was the bell one night and three people—one soldier with a gun, one civilian, and one woman—called us out.

I was in my room and my parents were in theirs. My husband wasn't at home. We were fetched from our beds. They sat us down in our hall and read a long paper which none of us understood, only *Arestovane . . . arestovane*, which means "arrest." That I understood. And then they said, "Ten minutes." They pointed at their watches and said, "Ten minutes." This was June 13, 1941.

After ten minutes they pushed us down the stairs. There was a wooden cart, the sort farmers used. They sat us in the cart and took us into the next street. Then a Russian officer came toward us and said, "Where are your things?" My mother, who could make herself un-

derstood in Ukrainian, said, "No one has said anything."
And he—he had such a sad face, even though he was a
Russian officer—he said, "All right. I will give you an
escort and you will go back to your flat and fetch everything you need. You will need it. You are going to Siberia."

So this was the first miracle, the first in a series of
miracles, which is why we are alive now.

I was the happy owner of two dictionaries, Russian-
German and German-Russian. I thought, "You will have
to learn Russian, Erika. There are no books in Russia, but
you have to learn Russian." So I took these two dictionaries and a rucksack, as if we were going for an outing.
I sat and cried, but my parents went back to the flat.
They had heard we would have to walk, so they didn't
take real things, only a jacket, a coat, a blanket—something warm. Then they put us into cattle wagons, not at
the main railway station but at a goods station. It was
said there were ten thousand of us, mainly Jews. Harm-
ful elements.

I don't know when the troubles began for me. Perhaps
in my schooldays in Austria, because until we were liberated by the Russians we belonged to Austria. My
town, Czernowitz, was near the border and in the First
World War my people fled to Vienna. But in Vienna
there was not enough food, and when I was seven I was
sent to school in a village in upper Austria. There were
six forms in the school and I was the only Jew. That was
my first year of schooling, and in that first year no other
child walked home from school with me. Twice a week

there was religious instruction—these were the children of Catholic farmers after all—and twice a week they would greet the priest, "Praised be Jesus Christ." This was the standard greeting. And I, a seven-year-old Jewish child from Vienna, was taught to say, "Küss die Hand." The priest never answered. I was there for a whole year and he never answered.

After school I would watch the oxen for the farmers, in return for that they allowed me to eat with them. Then in 1919 we came back to Czernowitz in Rumania. Twenty years later, on June 28, 1940, we were liberated and I saw my first Russian.

Many people fled. Many Jews and most of the Rumanians—the active Zionists, the estate owners— they fled. But those who wanted to work, the nameless ones like my father who were not afraid to work, they stayed. I don't remember hostility or fear. Of course we collected money for Palestine (grandfather was a Zionist), we gave money for planting trees. There was always the vision, the looking toward Palestine. One of my uncles went in 1935. But one had to be able to work with one's hands. I had friends who went—they built roads, but I was just a piano teacher and with me it was always my bad health. And I was an only daughter.

When the night hearings began I became uneasy.

One day, walking in the street, I met a friend. After the hearings ended we had all been given passports, a kind of identification paper known as a "58 Pass," and I said to this man, "What does it mean?" He said it means Siberia, that you are an enemy of the people. "Do something," he said. "Go and change it quickly, because this means Siberia." So we changed the bad passports and got good ones, and then we were arrested and put into cattle wagons and deported. I don't know to this day why we were arrested.

The wagons were for eight horses or forty men, and in our wagon we were more than a hundred. We were there for seventeen days. The whole trip from Czernowitz to our destination took two months. Once every three or four days they gave us something to eat. I don't know what we ate. Sometimes the farmers along the way gave us something. The first thing we bought was some sour milk in a stoneware jug in the Ural. Then one day there was a woman speaking German who walked along the train and called into the windows. You know the windows on a cattle wagon—small rectangles very high up, with metal bars? She called, "Does anybody here speak German?" We said, "Yes," and she said, "Do you know that we have been at war with Germany for four days?" We didn't know. We knew nothing. We had left on June 13 and it was now June 26, 1941. We saw only trainloads of soldiers going west—we went east and they went west. This we saw.

And then the children. Along the train, in the Ukraine, poor ragged children, running, calling *Chleba, chleba* ("bread, bread"). To us, to the prisoners who had nothing to eat, they called *chleba, chleba.* In the Ukraine, a rich country with wonderful soil, called the granary of Europe.

In the train we could look out of the windows, only they were high up and you had to stand on something. There was a girl, a very pretty girl who had just turned eighteen, and we used to send her to talk to the soldiers when the train stopped, to get us a little water. And I remember the day I had my thirtieth birthday. They gave me a present, a tin mug with water, so that I could wash. I was allowed to wash my face. That was my present.

The landscape? Very barren, except the Ural. The Ural is beautiful—mountains, a beautiful old city. In cities we were never in the main railway stations, we were always apart. We were enemies of the people and were heavily guarded. And then we were on a ship.

After seventeen days they loaded us onto a ship, not a ship for human beings, but a barge which is used to transport grain. We were pulled by a steamer, a real steamer with real people on board. There were these people up there on the steamer, with a salon and music. We could see each other. They saw us and we saw them, but they were afraid, afraid to talk to us. Even the people in the village where we finally arrived told us that before we came they had been called together and told "There are people coming who will appear very pleasant—clean and cultured. But you must be careful. These are enemies of the people and you must be very careful." But the people in Russia, even the farmers among whom we lived, very simple people but very Russian, didn't believe everything they were told. They were very patriotic, but not Communist. The expropriations, the transport to Siberia, the shootings, they went back to 1917. Stalin didn't come until 1926. We, of course, didn't know about this. But the farmers who had been there since the thirties told us that even then fathers and sons would be taken away and no one would hear of them again. So the people up there on the steamer, they were already used to seeing people like us, deportees. It was already part of the landscape.

The first ship could travel only on the river Ob. When we got to a tributary of the Ob, we were loaded onto a smaller ship—called a cutter, still quite a big boat, but with a roof and a ramp that ran around the outside. On this ramp father and I stood, day and night. There was no room to sit. My mother was ill, and I had a friend who had found a place for her to sit on the deck. She used to call me and I would climb up there and lie down for two or three hours every day. This is how we traveled for about a week. I don't know how we didn't fall into the water because, after all, we often fell asleep standing up, leaning against the roof which protected the grain. I suppose if we had fallen in someone would have pulled us out.

For days we traveled through what I think was a rain forest. Not a single house, nothing. Days and days on this river against the current. I remember at nights we were allowed to go on shore and then in the morning, very quickly, we could wash in the river. The water was dark brown. Sometimes it was impossible to land. It was jungle after all, primeval forest, so there were days when we couldn't land. It was July, not cold but it rained, so we were wet. Sometimes on land we could make a small fire, we could relieve ourselves. People were thirsty and they drank water from the river. It was dark brown, but they drank it. They fell ill. Most of us had dysentery.

We all got abscesses. My mother had such a terrible abscess and I begged to be allowed to boil some of the water on the bank. I remember the woman who was guarding us. She said, "Moscow does not believe your tears." It was a saying they had.

There were soldiers with us the whole way. Some were kind, they let us wash. We had things to eat—berries, and other things from the forest. In the villages when they loaded us from one ship to another sometimes we got food.

We came even deeper into the forest, to a village called Staritza. This was as far as a barge could go. Then we were on a smaller ship, and then on a still smaller ship—we were on a tributary of a tributary of a tributary. Finally we came to a river, which in summer is too shallow for ships, and we had to row ourselves. This was the last eight days. My father was one of the rowers—he had never had an oar in his hand before.

Some people had died already. An old woman died and ten men—we were Jews after all—ten men said the prayer one says over the dead and then they wrapped her in a sheet and threw her overboard into the water. After all we couldn't take along the dead. We never thought we would survive.

One day I saw a pig. Such happiness! I said to myself, That's a real pig, not a wild pig. So there must be people. We will survive. One of us, someone who spoke Russian, said, "We are now coming to a part of the country where there are people." I hadn't believed him until I saw the pig.

We came to the village of Pudino, in the Novosibirsk region. It isn't very far north, things grow there, potatoes and wheat. Nine months winter and three months summer, but a good summer. The guards called us all together. They sat at a table and we had to sign that we had voluntarily come to live here for twenty years. They translated it for me and then I ran crying to my mother. She was sitting there on all the bundles. She had this abscess. I told her what they had just said, and I remember her answering, "If they like, I can sign with them for fifty years." None of us believed we would live, none of us.

This was Siberia. Such poverty you thought existed only in a nightmare. And this was *before* the war. Industrious, hardworking, capable farmers, but such poverty! There was a farmer's wife who cut triangles out of old newspaper to make a curtain. An old shoebox was a treasure. Later we were like that, too, but I had never seen anything like it before. Their clothes weren't bought in a shop. Stalin had allowed them to spin a little flax, and they made clothes from that. Then they mended them, again and again. There were people who for years had only one change of clothes. I knew a woman who didn't have a shirt. She had a skirt and a blouse but no shirt, no underclothing. Of course there was no thread. We used to pull thread from the clothes we wore. Where we were staying there was a wooden floor, with wide gaps between the floor boards. And if the sewing needle fell, if you happened to drop the needle between the boards, your heart stood still because where would you get another needle?

My father had made friends with a woman in a shop, and she used to let him have some leaflets to use as paper, but now there was no paper. He said he would take my dictionary. "One can't be without paper," he said. "A man must have a piece of paper, how can one live without paper?" For nights I didn't sleep because I didn't know what I would do if my father took my dictionaries away from me. But he got some paper after all—thank God. There were the Communist propaganda brochures and he got those. And then he had paper.

Straight away we had lice. When one knows one has lice one can fight against them, one can catch them and kill them. But we didn't know. We knew that we itched but we didn't know it was lice.

My husband came. You remember, he wasn't there when we were arrested. My parents sent him a telegram. ERIKA IS ILL. They weren't allowed to tell the truth. And he came immediately, he volunteered to join us.

He first went back to our flat, but he couldn't get in. It had already been requisitioned. So he stayed with friends. The authorities wouldn't tell him where we were. There were several like him, who had hidden that night, who came. He first reached a village not far from us, about two hundred miles away. We found out by chance after nine months. You know how Jews are. There were people in Tashkent, a quite different region, who had fled from the Germans. Everybody was searching for relatives and wherever people were, whenever they wrote a letter, they included a list of those who were with them. So people found each other. That is how we heard that my husband was not far from us. And then he came.

We had come in August, he arrived in March. We had been married for five months and we were together another five months. He was with us from March until the following August. Then he fell ill with appendicitis. There was no doctor, no one to operate. So he died. That was in 1942.

In 1943 my father died of hunger. Whole families died of hunger and cold. There were farmers among us, Ukrainians and Rumanians—Rumanian farmers from small villages, people who still had family in Rumania —poor families without any possessions, with nothing. We thought they would live longest but they were the first who died. They couldn't adapt to the climate, couldn't learn the language. The local farmers laughed at them. Whole families died—in the first year the Rumanians and in the second year the Jews.

We lived with a Ukrainian farmer who had also been exiled. He and his family had already been there eleven years. They were exiled because—let's say because they had a tractor, or because they had cows and horses. So these were taken away from them and they were exiled. Among them were Germans who had come to live in the Ukraine in the nineteenth century. Most were exiled from Siberia itself, but from a good part of Siberia where they had gone voluntarily because the Csar promised them all the land they wanted, free. They had begun with nothing and in the end they had as many as a hundred cows. They were good farmers. And then in the thirties, with collectivization, they were exiled. They were sent across the marshes with their own horses when the marshes were still frozen, then the animals were taken from them and they had to work. They told us that when they arrived there was only snow and trees. They felled the trees and built themselves houses.

We were lucky. The first farmer we stayed with gave us a room, a sort of hall. For months we slept only on the floor. After three months they gave us a bed. It was a hall that opened directly to the outside. The water in the barrel used to freeze. And then in the winter the chickens stayed in the room with us, also the calf, sometimes a lamb—it was warmer that way. I worked in the *kolchoz,* picking and sorting flax, which meant we got a minimum amount of bread. We had to barter. We had no money but we bartered with things we had.

I don't know why we survived, my mother and I. I believe it was chance, only chance. Women survived more than men. Women seem to need less and they adapt more quickly. Even in the camps, people said, the men died before the women. Women need less food and are not required to work so hard.

We had a very kind, very humane commandant in the village. In the winter he left us alone. We had no winter clothes after all. And the local people didn't want us. "We don't want to work with Erika," they said. I had to dig potatoes and then lift the baskets onto a truck and they said I didn't lift hard enough. Probably I didn't, I was so weak. So I knitted. All winter I knitted.

They could knit, they knew how. Mittens, even gloves with fingers, socks. But they didn't know that one can knit a jacket or a sweater. They had two sheep, so there was wool, but I had no knitting needles.

There was a woman who had an umbrella. She took it apart and shared the spokes with me. So I had two knitting needles. They were terrible knitting needles, and the wool was terrible, too. But I knitted. I think we survived because of those knitting needles.

And then people began to know about me.

We could buy a little food, a little milk, and pay rent to the farmer we lived with. It was only the physical work we did that went to the *kolchoz.* We lived privately.

We each had a small patch of earth and this we could work, from this we lived. Winter was very hard. Thirty degrees below zero, sometimes more.

According to the plan, we were to start plowing on May 25 and finish on June 10. But very often we began on June 10 and finished on June 25. Everything has to be planted quickly because summer is so short. The fields were covered mostly with weeds since the war had already begun and there were no horses to plow with. The horses had died of hunger. And no oxen. So we plowed with cows, even with women—eight women in one plow. I was digging with another woman, in new earth. One person alone couldn't push the spade into the ground. With two feet you could.

In the first year we got no grain at all. Later for one day's work we got one glass of grain, most of it was straw. Perhaps a quarter of it was grain. It used to take me four or five days work to fulfill my day's quota. I couldn't keep up, so they brought me before a court and tried me.

But you see the local people were humane, they saw that I was trying but that I was really not strong enough. And already my knitting was not unimportant to them. Mama had found something to unravel and so we had colored yarn which we crocheted around the collar and sleeves. They were very impressed. Mama had also brought a sewing kit and we had a few buttons. A button!

Gradually I became the *kolchoz* seamstress. First I knitted by the light of the fire. We had no other lights and it grew dark early. Then I started to sew. Not because I knew how but from necessity. First I made a blouse out of my late husband's jacket. Then the teacher said to me, "This thing you made for yourself, make me one, too." So I began to take old clothes apart and make new things from them. This is why they defended me before the court—·so I shouldn't have to do black work, so I would be allowed to sew. This was in 1946.

The first time we had news from the outside world was from Palestine in 1944. We had relatives there, not near relatives, but they were relatives. There were letters and then right away a parcel, two parcels. That was also the year we got our first hut.

A woman, a neighbor of ours, had decided to flee. This was possible if you knew how. She was a very pretty young woman with a young boy and was the wife of a member of the Red Army. She was also the mistress of the manager and others. People knew she wanted to flee. And one could flee in winter, across the marshes, because in winter the marshes were frozen. It was over seven miles to the beginning of the marshes and then another thirty miles, quite flat, with low trees and low bushes growing, across the marshes. There was a path that hunters used to take. There were a few hunters, a few elk. It was illegal to shoot elk but they did. Otherwise there was meat only when the farmers killed a pig, then if you had something to barter you might get some of the innards. One ate whatever one could. People said they found mice and rats in the stomachs of those who had starved to death. So in winter there was a path. The militia had a hut there to make sure that people didn't escape, but our neighbor escaped. And we got her hut. Actually, I traded my coat for the hut.

Just recently I dreamed about this hut. It had a wooden fence surrounding the garden, the garden that we lived on. In my dream two horses broke the fence and came into the garden. We were growing potatoes. One of the horses didn't trample the potatoes but lay on its back and rolled back and forth, back and forth over them. I was desperate because these were our potatoes, our food for the whole year. In my dream I cried so bitterly that when I woke up I was bathed in sweat.

But this is what really happened. I told you my father died of hunger, yet one doesn't just die from hunger. In 1942, the crops failed and we had nothing to barter, nothing to sell. Potatoes have to be dry. But the potatoes were planted on moorland, and when it rained, they rotted. So there was nothing. As a young man my father had had pneumonia. He coughed a lot and just wasted away. Again, there was no doctor, only a midwife. There was a doctor thirty-seven miles away, but that was a journey of three days.

You only die of hunger in February and March. In summer there is always something, grass—something. But in the summer, in August, my husband died of appendicitis. He came home from work one day very ill. My mother went to the nurse and asked her to come, but she wouldn't. Then my mother took her a present, a shawl, and she came. She looked at his stomach, I don't know what she did. That was in the afternoon. In the evening he was dead.

Yes, we had a graveyard. The farmers had a graveyard and they gave us, the Jews, a small piece of ground. My father died in March. March 29. We found a man, we gave him some things—my father's trousers—and he kept a fire going for two days, two nights. This fire first thawed the snow and then the frozen ground. But, with just one man digging, the grave was still very shallow. They told us how in spring and summer the dogs would dig up the bones. We put small wooden slats into the ground around the grave, but they fell down since the soil was not real soil.

There were some who committed suicide, who hanged themselves, but relatively few. There was a narrow wooden plank on which I had to cross the river on the way to work and I alway used to think, why not? Why not jump, make an end to it? But I didn't.

If Stalin had not died in 1953, we would all have died. This is quite, quite certain. It was like the difference between night and day when Stalin died and Khrushchev took over. It took about a year after Stalin died and then, after 1954, we weren't so hungry anymore. We had a different hut and a different garden with better soil. Better soil means better potatoes. It wasn't so bad after that. And after 1954, we were allowed contact with Israel.

We had had contact in 1944, but this was with Palestine, not *Israel.* It seemed so very far away, and the relatives we had were not near relatives. Also there was always the feeling of being arrested again. I always said that I did not want anything from life except this: That if I have never stolen and never committed murder, I should not have to be afraid all the time of prison, of being arrested. One was eternally arrested or deported, and didn't know why. People were arrested every day.

We had contact with Palestine—in '44, '45, '46, '47. But after the founding of the state in '48, people who had contact with Israel were arrested as spies for America or England and sentenced to ten years, fifteen years, twenty years. Mainly men. A friend of ours was sentenced to eight years for having contact with Israel. Until the last moment you were due to be freed, you never knew whether you would be arrested again.

We were freed after seventeen years. That is to say, we had to sign again—one always had to sign—that we would never again return to our home, that we would never ask that our property be returned. This was in 1958. I still have the documents relinquishing my "rights of citizenship." So I went to Tomsk, the nearest town, four hundred miles away, with these documents, to get work so we would have money to get to Israel.

But in 1958 there was no work in Tomsk. You couldn't get work if you did not have a flat and you couldn't get a flat if you did not have work. I stayed for eight days. There were already many people in Tomsk and long queues for everything, and I saw that life there was much more difficult than in the village of Pudino. So we went back to the village.

We already had our fourth hut and a few chairs and the door didn't freeze shut anymore in winter. It was already human then. And we had help from Israel. People were allowed to send us parcels of dark blue cloth, in lengths, and these we could barter with the military. There were two of us, mother and I, so we were allowed a garden. And since I was the seamstress and almost fifty-five, I didn't have to work as much anymore.

Three years before, in '55, I had begun to apply to go to Israel. We read once in a newspaper that Austrian citizens could be repatriated. I applied to the Austrian consul in Moscow. His reply was very sympathetic, but the letter ended, "In your case, I imagine, emigration will be difficult." He realized where we were.

I did nothing more about it. I suppose we could have gone to Austria, just to get out, but I never thought of any country except Israel. When after two thousand years you suddenly have a state for Jews, you want to be with your people. It was perhaps in 1962—we didn't have a radio until 1961—that I first heard a Jewish song on the radio. It was such an event. I cried and cried. Why were young people all over the world allowed to live with their friends and families while my mother and I had to live in this wilderness? I don't want to say anything against the people of Siberia. The Russians are human, too, but they are strangers. When I applied to leave, everybody laughed at me. "They won't let you go."

Did the other Jews want to go? In the end there was only my mother and me, and one other woman and her daughters. Most of the others had died. Some went to the bigger villages and even there they died. There was a time when young people who had been only fifteen or so when they were transported were given permission to leave, and then they were arrested again. A few got away. This other woman applied to return to her home in Bessarabia, but we never wanted to return. There was no one there anymore. So I applied for Israel. What could I lose? Where could they exile me? I was already at the end of the earth.

We applied once and were refused. Then the second time—it wasn't easy. Just the photographs: somewhere in Russia there are sixty-four photographs of my mother and sixty-four photographs of me, I imagine in all the criminal files. We were criminals, enemies of the people.

A student came and took photographs. The nights it cost, the thinking and planning! Once there was a photographer, a real one, and my mother put on our jacket, the one we had been sharing, and made herself beautiful for the photograph so that we could show our relatives in Israel what she looked like. When our applications were turned down, we were convinced we wouldn't see them again. It was just a dream. They turned down the first application. And then the second. The third, and the fourth. The relatives had to beg, in Russian, to explain that the entire family had been wiped out by the Nazis, that there were just the two of us, two women, alone and old—that we wouldn't become a burden on the state, that they should allow us to join our family. And then, in 1963, they gave us permission.

I remember going to tell my mother. It was August, the beginning of the potato harvest, and she was in the cellar under the floor. Every August Mama cleaned out the cellar for the potatoes. She put her head out of the trapdoor and I told her the news. She couldn't believe it. She said to me, "Erika, Erika, you are losing your reason."

There was a Russian woman with me, an official—the news had come by post. I was a little confused myself, and then right away the militia came and said, "Three days." We had to leave within three days. The people were furious. They said, "You keep them here for twenty-two years and then give them three days to leave! Do you have to treat them like criminals?" And one of the Russians, he had been through a lot himself, kept saying, "We are one people, one people. Yet people are so different." So we had three days.

We liquidated everything—it was a little house after

all—and distributed presents. There was no time to pack things. After three days they put us on a truck. We went six miles with the truck and then we were put on a small airplane. We flew to the next town. Then we got into a bigger plane and flew to the center of the region. We had to go to the militia to sign out and were given a kind of intermediate passport. Even though we had been set free we were not real citizens. Then we got on a ship going downstream, as far as Tomsk. We were on the ship, in a cabin, like human beings, for twenty-four hours. It had been twenty-two years after all. So many dead, and all the graves remained behind. Here now, just the two of us, a kind of miracle.

In Tomsk I had to go to the militia again. "You're crazy," the official said. "These things take months, go back." It was always like this. But one can't go back.

Someone found us a hotel, and the real miracle was that we discovered that we had money. We had saved a little, every penny, but now we found that we had money from relatives who had been repatriated to Poland. There was also the money we had paid to the state in taxes, a sort of compulsory loan, and when they struck us off the register, when we were no longer citizens, they paid this back.

So they paid us back this sum. The official said, "What are you going to do with this money?" It was a hundred rubles. I said, "I will buy a coat. I will buy a coat because I don't want people to see I have come from Siberia." He liked that. They like you to make a good impression.

We had to wait three months in Tomsk, and in the end I didn't know whether I would get the papers. We were told, "No. You have seen things, you have heard things, you know too much. You could harm us." That night I didn't sleep. I kept thinking, Where can I go with my mother?—she was seventy-eight. Then the next morning we got the passports.

They were still Soviet passports, not international passports. I didn't get the international passports until I got to Moscow. And in Moscow they treated us like criminals again, like traitors. They searched everything. My mother couldn't bring herself to part with anything, not the smallest apron, and they searched it all—shoes, the heels of shoes, the hand luggage. And in Kiev they took us off the plane and searched us again. The flight to Austria took four hours. About an hour after we took off I said to my mother, very quietly, "I hope the clouds below us are already Hungarian clouds." But it was only when I stepped off the plane in Vienna . . . you see, you never knew. So many people, they took them off ships, they took them off planes—even those who already had papers. It was only when I stepped off the plane in Vienna that I knew we were free.

And then there, straight away, the anti-Semitism again.

Vienna had a special significance for us. We had lived there for four years and loved it. The Emperor Franz Josef had been good to the Jews. Even my German sounds a little Viennese.

I said to Mama, "Let's buy a postcard."

The man who sold us the postcard was very friendly, so I asked him how much the postage to Israel was. The moment I said Israel his face turned to ice. I thought to myself, How good it is that we don't have to stay.

In Russia schoolchildren are taught that Israel has no bread, that everyone is hungry. I thought everyone would be poor. On the ship coming to Haifa they gave us apples. My mother said, "I am sure the children in Israel have never seen apples." So we saved the apples and brought them for the children. You see this gold ring I am wearing? There was a woman who shared a room with us in the hotel in Tomsk while we were waiting for our papers. When we said we were going to Israel she cried, because she said we would be hungry. She gave me this gold ring, it had belonged to her grandmother. She said it would make her happy if we took it and sold it, so that for perhaps just one day we would not starve in Israel.

And then we arrived, and I saw fruit—all the fruit in December—and the cars, and the clothes people wore. In those first months I kept thinking to myself: This is how they have been living here and that is how we had been living there. It seemed not entirely just.

But the welcome! We arrived in Haifa on December 15, 1963. They were so *loving*, even strangers shared everything with us. A man from the Jewish Agency stood up and came over to me and he said, "I must shake the hand of a woman who has been in Siberia for twenty-two years. I must wish her luck."

There is a Jewish song about the unknown poor relative to whom you must show kindness. I had imagined it like that. Although I had written the postcard from Vienna, I didn't think it would have arrived. I had imagined that in December, winter, it would be raining. I said to Mama, "No one will know we are coming."

But such a reception, so many people, friends. Friends who after twenty-two years had taken a day off to come to Haifa.

The presents, and a flat—right away, on the first day. I felt like a queen. They said, "You can live anywhere you like, Tel Aviv, Haifa, Kiriat Tivon. . . ." But we wanted to be in Jerusalem.

That night we were gathered up by my father's sister-in-law. Her husband had died years before, she had no duty toward us, but she said, "You are staying with us." But a friend who had a ticket to a concert that night had heard that I used to be a musician. She said, "You are going to the concert. I will stay at home and prepare a bath for you and you will go to the concert with my husband." That my first night in Israel should begin with music! She wasn't even a close friend. I didn't speak Hebrew and I didn't have a job, but right away I was at home. I shall never forget that concert. The London Symphony Orchestra played "Hatikvah," our national anthem. My friend's husband, who was sitting beside me, turned to me and said, "That I should live to hear an English orchestra play "Hatikvah." . . . He had been in Palestine during the days of the British mandate.

Next door to us is a family of Jews from America. They are very pious and every Shabbat they go to schul with their prayer shawls, with the talis, the boy children all with long sidelocks. For a long time I could not get over it, that one could walk like this through the streets, freely.

There are things my mother still does—I must tell you. Everywhere, on every shelf, we have old newspapers and magazines. My mother can't bear to throw them out. Once I remember walking along the street and seeing a dirty rag, a piece of cloth somebody had thrown out. We took it home and washed and mended it, every hole. But it is terrible this thing about newspapers. I had to tell my mother that blind people sell newspapers, then she felt better about treating herself to a newspaper. I once saw a child throw away a falafel and I almost burst into tears.

We are better now, but there was a time when my mother used to collect the pieces of stale bread that people had thrown out and take them to the lambs. We have lambs in the valley below us.

4

Sylva Zalmanson

"If we stay we'll be arrested," he said. "We've got too much education." We were trapped like spiders in a jar.

I had already tried to emigrate twice. Once in 1968, and then two years later. Now again we had an invitation from my uncle who was already in Israel. We had all applied—me, twenty-two years old; Edward, my husband of two weeks; and my two brothers, Wulf and Izrail. We couldn't get the character reference.

I had a degree in engineering. I was working in a factory, designing machines. When I went to my boss, the director of the plant, he asked why I wanted a character reference. "To get a visa. The emigration authorities insist."

"Yes," he said. "But I am not obliged." He was right —he was not obliged. They insist, and he is not obliged.

Edward went from Riga, my hometown, to Moscow, then to Strunino, then back to Riga to try to get a reference. In Riga the chairman of the hospital where he was working said, "Why are you going to Israel?" Then suddenly, "What would happen if my son was sent to fight for the Arabs, what would you do? Shoot him?" Naturally he didn't get a character reference.

Wulf was refused a reference because he was in the army, Izrail because he was still a student, me because I was "no longer a student." The reasons given never have anything to do with Israel. Take Mikhail, one of our group. His family vanished in 1944, when he was a child, and a few years later he heard that they were alive and living in Israel. He had been trying to join them for twenty years.

In itself the reference is not difficult to obtain, but once it is known that you want to emigrate to Israel you are denied everything. So now we became desperate.

Butman had come from Leningrad to Riga to tell me about his plan to steal a plane. I didn't say anything to my husband at first, but I did tell Wulf. He was skeptical. "It's a gamble—a hopeless gamble." Wulf's situation was more hopeless than anybody's because as a mechanical engineer and an army officer he still had fifteen years to serve. But Izrail was excited. There had just recently been a plane escape from Poland to the west. "What about us? Why can't we do that?" Izrail had said. At the time we just laughed at him, but by now I, too, was willing. So when Butman came a second time, I agreed to talk with my husband.

Edward was only half Jewish. He had grown up ignorant of Jewish culture. But Edward was more experienced than any of us. I met him in Leningrad where he had just spent seven years in prison. He told me that while in jail he had decided that if he was ever released he would go to Israel if he had to walk all the way, even if it meant going illegally. Even, he said, if it meant being arrested again. As it turned out, this was a kind of prophecy.

Finally we were all agreed on a plan, although we did not all agree that we would succeed. Edward talked to the pilot. We continued to meet secretly, both in Leningrad and in the Rumbula Forest outside Riga. In a forest it is easy to see if you are being followed.

Everything had begun in the Rumbula Forest. In the beginning all there was was a big pit and nothing to show it was a Jewish grave. A memorial said SOVIET CITIZENS, which was meaningless when you think that thirty-seven thousand people were killed there by the Nazis not because they were Soviet citizens but because they were Jews. Only Jews died here, but how do you convey this if you cannot write the word *Jew*? If you wrote it in Hebrew it would be understood, but Hebrew was forbidden. Finally it was permitted to write HERE LIE CITIZENS in Yiddish. If it was written in Yiddish, it meant Jewish citizens.

At Rumbula I met young Jews who had grown up in Riga, but had never known about the Holocaust even though they had relatives lying there. This was horrifying to me.

Every weekend people came to gather up the bones and fragments to make a proper cemetery. It took years, but was already done when I arrived. We went in hundreds every Sunday to pay homage. The Russians would stand in the trees and jeer, shouting, "They didn't kill enough of you." There was never a big quarrel between the Nazis and the Soviet authorities about the Jewish question.

Rumbula was where all my friendships began. At

school I didn't have friends. I was the only Jewish person in a special school for the sick—I'd had tuberculosis—and as soon as I came the other students called me a Jew and started to hit me. I was beaten every day, and the teachers never interfered. The Latvians are not nice people.

Through my Rumbula friends I met Butman's people in Leningrad. They had a group and I began distributing Hebrew literature for them. Some of us were only children, but—this is when I got excited—I was able to learn Hebrew, although it was officially forbidden. Everything about Israel except the official line in *Pravda* was forbidden. Any statistics, any facts, any information. You could learn Hebrew by yourself, but it was forbidden to use a book not published in Russia, and since there were no Russian books in Hebrew, how could you learn it if it was forbidden to find a teacher? So we typed our own books in order to learn. I can't define the feeling—half excited and always afraid—and even now I speak in Hebrew with great pleasure. Suddenly it was all so clear. In Russia nothing was ours—not the vastness of the country, not the heroes, not the Russian language. We were a strange element. Even though our parents and grandparents were born there, it wasn't the same. Not even Russian literature helped. Even the big names— Gogol, Dostoevski—are anti-Semitic. And the feeling you don't belong—you didn't belong yesterday and you won't belong tomorrow and your children won't belong —you're like an orphan. And all of a sudden, this language: you find your parents. This is why Hebrew was so important.

All my life I felt that to be Latvian was good, to be

Russian was good, but to be Jewish meant something was wrong with you. I've forgotten all the insults except for one very funny one when I was sitting on a beach, and a young, very friendly fellow sat down beside me. "What's your name?" he said. I wouldn't say. I didn't like him. But he was persistent. "What nationality are you?" My name I wouldn't say, but this I had to answer. Anyway, I don't look Latvian, I look Jewish. "I'm Jewish," I said. "Oh, I'm sorry," he said, "I didn't mean it that way."

If you went to borrow a book you had to fill out a library card with the question "Nationality?" Everywhere you were reminded of it, that you were different.

We were running an underground magazine, an account of the Six Day War. We printed anything we could find about Israel. I made photocopies. I hid them at home in old picture albums because I didn't want Father to be worried. You can't do it openly in a communal apartment with three families sharing a kitchen. You might as well do it in the backyard of the K.G.B. A member of the group borrowed a friend's room saying he wanted to bring his mistress. That's where he copied the stuff. My brothers helped, we were all in it.

We had already sent an appeal to the West, saying, "We are just some of the tens of thousands of Jews who are denied the right to emigrate." We sent letters all over the world. Nothing. There was no response. You know when it is you begin to feel frightened in Russia? When things are quiet.

I didn't say anything to Father or to Samuel, my third brother. Father thought about Israel in traditional ways —"Next year in Jerusalem," but no more than that.

Samuel's fiancée would never have worked for our cause, and we couldn't risk her knowing anything.

"Even if we fail," Butman said, "it will mean a scandal and a chance for thousands of others." But as the time drew near, he backed out. It was only when Edward joined us and took over the planning with the pilot that anything happened. For the first time things looked hopeful. We decided to escape in May.

At first we talked of hijacking a plane in the air, but there were too many of us, sixteen altogether. Then we thought of stealing a plane from Smolny, the Leningrad airport. I went there at night and found the airport lit by searchlights, with dogs everywhere, so this too was abandoned. The final plan, the one Edward worked out, was to buy all the seats on a regular commercial flight for Finland and, once we had taken off, to overpower the pilot and fly straight to Sweden. "No violence," Edward stressed.

We gave up jobs, hobbies, studies, everything. For weeks we talked of nothing but freedom, but it was strange how depressed I became. I was dreaming a lot, and all my dreams said we would fail. In one dream I was in a room with my husband. He tied me up and went into the next room. That was all. I said to Edward, "We won't take off." "Why?" he said. "I keep having this dream, the same one. Over and over," I told him. "It's only a dream." He laughed it off.

We bought the tickets and were to leave on May 2. But on April 29 Butman phoned from Leningrad to say it was off. I didn't understand. He said his contact in Israel had advised us to wait. So we fixed a new date for June 15.

We signed a testimony explaining our motives and posted it abroad in case we were killed. Wulf left a note for Father in the television set, but I think I must have had a premonition we were being watched because instead of leaving a note in the house I gave mine to a friend to give to my father. As it turned out, he didn't give it to him.

We went by train to Leningrad and there Edward noticed we were being followed. We had left some luggage at the station, and when we opened it we saw that it had been searched. Edward said, "There's no going back." He had this burning desire for freedom. By now our dream of getting to Israel was stronger than any fear. Wulf had deserted from the army—for him it was all or nothing. We divided into two groups, twelve and four.

The main group would board the plane at Smolny as planned. Edward went with this group. The men were to overpower the pilot and co-pilot and put them down at an intermediate airport called Priozersk, where four of us, including me, would be waiting.

Priozersk is north of Leningrad, I'm not sure how far north. It is a small airport in a forest about half an hour's flying time from Sweden. We reached the forest after midnight, maybe two in the morning. The trees had a softening, soothing effect, and I remember the aroma of the pine needles before we fell asleep.

We were dressed as hikers. If we were caught we would say we were on a picnic.

I realized we would be arrested. Coming from Leningrad in the train we could see we were being followed. We changed trains twice. I kept telling myself it was suicide, but we knew all along that it was necessary to commit an illegal act, a deliberate illegal act. It's like beating your head against a wall, but in such a way that somebody has got to pay attention. Yet, on looking back, I can see that maybe some small place inside me still believed in a miracle because I had brought with me some photographs from home and a letter from my mother.

It was quiet in the pines. We didn't say much. Just before we fell asleep Boris said, "It's so good to be free."

We were sleeping when they came. "Hands up," they said. No questions. We were taken to the nearest police station and charged with treason. They asked us to sign a protocol statement saying that in attempting to cross the border without permission we were guilty of treason against the Soviet Union. We refused.

We learned later that Edward and the others had reached the airport at Smolny. They checked in and waited until the flight was called. They were allowed through the barrier onto the tarmac. They were arrested as they walked across the tarmac to board the plane.

"Russia disgusts you, doesn't it?" one of the guards said to me. The K.G.B. men who arrested us kept saying, "Why did you do it?" And this one guard answered for us, "It's not because you love Israel, you don't know Israel. It's because you hate what's here, isn't it, Russia disgusts you. *Disgusts* you." But I think he said that because it is what he felt.

They knew everything. They had heard our conversations on the telephone; any dialogue indoors in apartments had been recorded; they found Wulf's note in the television set. And in court they produced a copy of the testimony we had sent to the West that had our names and signatures on it.

Perhaps we lied to ourselves, perhaps it wasn't possible. We hadn't even found the airport. In the forest at Priozersk we decided to go to sleep and get up early and look for it the next day, but maybe we wouldn't have found it the next day either. We had never been there before. During the trial we grew up, but before that I think some of us were playing a game, like children. Pretending to be hikers! I was carrying a rucksack, but I was wearing a raincoat and shoes with high heels and carrying an umbrella. Mary's husband was wearing a track suit and hiking boots, but he was also carrying a white suitcase. It was almost funny. And the K.G.B. trailing us were dressed in the same silly fashion.

Ten of them, ten people with dogs, arrested the four of us.

We weren't armed. One man had a toy pistol to frighten the pilot and co-pilot, and another had a pistol he had made himself which didn't work. Even the interrogators laughed when they examined the pistol.

What we didn't know, because the early interrogations were secret, was what had become of the original testimony we had posted abroad. We had asked that it be made public at the hour the plane was due in the air. The interrogations went on for days, months. I did not see Edward again until the trial began in Leningrad in December. The prosecutor demanded the death sentence. He said it was a criminal trial and had nothing to do with Jews. He said the Soviet people were incapable of anti-Semitism. It wasn't until the very end, when the sentences were announced, that we knew anything. We had no news. We thought we had failed.

The prosecutor was a well-known anti-Semite. He said to Murzhenko, one of the group, whom he wanted to shame, "You, a *Ukrainian*, you want to go to a Jewish country!" And Murzhenko said, "No, I didn't. I wanted to go to India." Look. When you stand on trial in Russia, everybody is frightened.

When Edward and I saw each other again, we were overjoyed. And when our relatives in the court spotted us, they began to cry. We were tried separately. When I was called as a witness to the trial of Ruth Alexandrovich, she was so unhappy that I tried to pick up her spirits by making a face at her. She looked at me and broke down. Then I wanted to cry, because she had lost so much weight.

Only the Russian press was allowed in. We had to stand with our shoulders back, to keep good posture. We admitted trying to cross the frontier illegally, but not treason.

So many charges. I can't remember them all. One accused us of misappropriating government property "of particularly large dimensions." We had a lawyer. He was a Russian lawyer, a good lawyer, but it was a formality. There was never a case of a lawyer getting anyone off in Russia.

When the witnesses—the relatives—were called, they took it seriously. Being on oath, they told the truth and said how they felt. When the prosecutor asked why we wanted to escape, for example, they said, "Well, life is better there." It was their explanation and in this explanation you could see just what they thought of the Soviet Union. Fyodor's mother was called. Fyodor had told his mother that he thought he was being watched, but she'd said to pay no attention. In court she exactly repeated what she had told him, "Pay no attention, son. Pay no attention at all, Fyodor, because in Russia *everybody is being watched.*"

I could see my father, he was so hurt. He was shaking. Samuel told me afterward that at first Father didn't know where we were. After the K.G.B. had searched and found Wulf's note, Father thought that because there was no news we'd escaped, and he began crying, "They're heroes, they're heroes!" Then when he heard of the arrest he became angry and blamed Edward for abducting his children without permission. "My three children," he said. Poor Father, he was so mixed up.

They allow you a final plea before the sentences are pronounced. I don't remember what I said when my turn came. Except for our relatives, all the people in the courtroom were members of the K.G.B. in civil dress. The whole atmosphere was hostile, yet when I spoke I felt that somebody was in sympathy. They seemed to listen. It was very quiet. I remember that I was speaking in Russian and then suddenly I broke into Hebrew: *Im esh kahech Yerushalayim tishkach yemini* ("If I forget thee, O Jerusalem, let my right hand lose her cunning!"). I was speaking into a microphone. I didn't get far because the judge stopped me. He said, "It is forbidden to speak in a foreign language." I don't think he understood what I was saying, but Edward did. He threw me a look and put his hand up to his head as if to say, "My God, woman.

What have you done?" He thought it would finish me. But then a woman sitting just below me blew me a kiss. So I'm glad I said it.

We were given long sentences. Edward and the pilot were sentenced to death. When the sentences were announced the public applauded. I was stunned.

Nothing was said in court, but in the newspapers it was written that we had intended to kill the pilot and co-pilot. The papers used words like *bandits* and *terrorists,* to describe us, "agents of Shin Bet." But the journalists were obliged to write what they did.

Father was allowed to see me for half an hour before we went back to prison. We were taken first to prison and then to labor camps. He told me very quickly in Yiddish that the world knew. That people were talking about our case, that our trial was a show trial and there were already protests abroad. He said it had begun in New York when Meir Kahane, the American rabbi, went to the Soviet Embassy and started breaking windows. This had been published in the Russian press.

Such a difference it made, to know that we were not alone. It was the first indication that people cared.

Later, when he came to see me in the labor camp, Father said that young people were now being allowed to leave Russia. More than a hundred thousand of them —from Riga, from Moscow, from Leningrad, from Minsk, from Odessa, from Kiev, from Lithuania, from many parts—have left so far. Nearly all are in Israel now.

All my life I have loved this country, loved it even in my dreams. Before I was released from prison I remember getting a letter from someone in Israel telling me about the places she had seen and the Wall, the Western

Wall. Oh Jerusalem, I thought, and Tel Aviv at night. But when she described the skirts and shoes in the latest fashion, then I really got excited—I wanted so much to be there.

When I read the reaction to my husband's death sentence in one of the Russian newspapers, I thought it was all over for him. I wanted so much to see him, but then I thought that even if he has not seen the paper he would be able to tell from my face that his life was finished. I found out later that I would not have been allowed to see him anyway. But we appealed to the high court and within a week we were told that the death sentences for my husband and the pilot were commuted to fifteen years—because of the reaction abroad. Because of that only.

In his book, the one he wrote in prison that was smuggled out, Edward says I looked ill and that I was smoking too much. I was able to see him once for an hour. Later I tried to send him food. His camp, where he is still, was separate from mine. It is a hard labor camp with criminals. The regime is as strict as it can be. But maybe for us in the women's camp conditions were not so different. Everyone was ill from the food—food and nerves. I fasted twice a year. On the anniversary of the arrest and of the sentencing. The whole group did. Abroad many people fasted with us in sympathy.

It's funny about smoking. My mother used to smoke and I very much liked the smell. But I said to her once, "I don't want to start because if I go to prison I won't be able to get any cigarettes." I was about fifteen when I said this. But then in prison I found you could get a very heavy tobacco and make your own cigarettes. I started to smoke and I smoked nonstop.

After a year I realized there was an informer in my cell. I was naive not to realize sooner. I learned many things in prison, things I had only read about in books. You feel a need to know what the prison experience is like because prison is so much a part of life in Russia. In prison you always have to define yourself between the prisoners and the guards. You are with one or the other. In between are the little people. My husband writes of this in his book. He writes of Liapchenko, the little anti-Semite standing with the lighted brushwood in his hand, waiting to see how the wind blows, the little collaborator who worked with Nazis and then with the K.G.B. because he was unable to resist. Just an ordinary little man.

At first I didn't want to believe that this woman was a spy. Once she said to me, "It's a pity Hitler didn't kill all of you," and because I was waiting for a meeting with my husband I didn't hit her.

During the hour we had together, we talked a little about what we were reading—we had been reading so much. I was reading Spinoza. There we were, in just that one precious hour that was given to us in Edward's camp, discussing Spinoza's definition of liberty!

I began to read philosophy in prison because it helped me to understand my husband. It made me feel closer to him. He had been studying philosophy for many years, but for me it was difficult. We had only been married five months before the arrest. He still has eight years to go. There are a hundred of them in his camp, but only about ten are political prisoners. My brothers Wulf and

Izrail are also in camps. Wulf received fifteen years and Izrail ten years, the same as I got.

One day when I was sewing gloves I was taken away from the camp without any warning. I had been there four years and at first I thought I would see him again, because I had been asking for another meeting for a long time. But when we passed my husband's camp without stopping I began to worry; I thought I might be getting a harder sentence. They took me to another prison and kept me a week without saying anything.

And then I was free—given amnesty. I didn't shout or shake. My face became paralyzed. I said, "Who asked for this mercy? I didn't ask for mercy."

They said I could go to Israel, they even insisted I go to Israel. Why me and not the others? They told me I must be out in three weeks. They said I could not see my husband. I insisted. They said if I insisted, they would put me back in prison. But I said, "I refuse to leave unless I can see him." I wanted to wait for him in Russia. I was willing to wait and wait.

In the end we were together for five days. I was taken to Moscow, and he was brought there from his camp. We were together in a cell. I told him that friends had advised me not to wait. I was uncertain. He said, "Go while you can." I didn't know what was right. I thought by staying I would be able to save him. He told me not to be crazy. "It is not in your power to save me," he said. "They are letting you go because of the fuss abroad. You are popular now, but it won't always be so." He was right.

When I arrived in Israel, people asked, "Where are you working?" "Where are you living?" I was suspicious. I didn't like these questions. Even in America, where I once went on a visit, the first question was, "What is your name?" Second question, "What are you doing?" I always said something vague.

It took a year before I lost this suspicion, the feeling that I was being followed, that the telephone was tapped. When I came to the apartment, I had a security lock put on my door. I was so nervous I would jump at the slightest sound. Now it's better. You will think it strange, but I am not ashamed to say that the first thing I did when I came to Israel was to buy a pair of shoes. Bright yellow shoes.

Now I need quiet things. Recently, when I was ill, I needed people. I was working—I work as an engineer in the aircraft industry (but I am not allowed to say what I do)—and I was traveling to England and America a lot, lecturing and talking about the ones who cannot leave because in Russia the position is again hard, the situation is again serious. There are still three million Jews there. They let out some and not others; there is no reason to it. Many dissidents have been arrested again. In America I went on a long hunger strike so I could go back and join my husband, but it didn't work. After that I was ill. Pneumonia leaves you feeling weak. Many people visited me, but for a long time afterward I remained here in the apartment. I couldn't bring myself to visit them back.

I miss my friends, but they are in Russia. It is as if everything is in the past.

Do you know Achmatova? In one of her poems she says that we remember everything that is in the past.

Then we go back and everything is dusty and there are cobwebs in the corners. We wash our hands. Suddenly there are no weaknesses in the past. No people you can cry with or remember with. And if God has separated you from your friends, you feel you can do without them.

And maybe it is better.

It was in the paper yesterday that my brother Samuel has been arrested on a charge of taking bribes. Now they are all in camps. It is something to live with.

The ordinary Soviet citizen has his complaints. Sometimes there is sausage in the shops and sometimes there isn't. But essentially when it comes to Jews and Israel he sides with the authorities. It's a very sad thing to say, but in general the public is anti-Semitic. If there are no longer any pogroms, it is because it isn't done that way anymore. It is not that the government is anti-Semitic and the people are neutral: they both agree on it.

It's not only Jews, it happens to any minority group. In my camp were the followers of Bender, the Ukrainian nationalist. Natasha, one of the Ukrainian women, used to join me in my hunger strikes, and when her group fasted, I joined them. It's like the Czech rising in '67 when the Russians sent in tanks—the moment a different group or a different culture is involved, the public supports the authorities: *"It has to be done,"* they say. Educated people say this. Do you know that they cannot define Zionism?

Zionism. What is it? For me it is returning. It is returning after being driven out. But the Russians say Zionism is a running sore on the face of decadent imperialism. They also say this about art, about anything that is contrary to the official line. The ordinary person can never know what it is about. It is like the definition of a god. "He is not like this and not like that," but what he is nobody knows.

I think now if I had stayed in Russia I could have done more to help my husband. In Israel I am regarded as a bit of a troublemaker. As my grandmother said, I am not very "ladylike." Maybe they expect me to sit at home quietly and say nothing. Now I am sitting quietly because I feel the strain and it is difficult to go on fighting every day.

Edward is stronger than I am. He identifies with Jews because he understands our fate, to be always under the pressure of evil. In court, when the prosecutor asked him for his nationality, he said, "I am a Jewish citizen. I was born a citizen of the state of Israel." And he is half Russian. I remember in a dream I spoke to his father. I said, "Will he be happy?" The answer came, "He will never be happy." I think he suffers. It is very Russian, yes—very Russian. And very Jewish, too.

I hope he will like it when he comes. Here, even if you don't do anything, you feel you are taking part in something good. But eight years. It is a lot of time to destroy a young man.

I get letters from him, one letter every two months. I can write more often, but the letters will not reach him. And sometimes I cannot write.

I am very comfortable now. I don't think about who I am. I enjoy many little pleasures, like lying in bed late or drinking coffee. In prison there wasn't any coffee.

I lie on the bed and I don't think any more about who I am—I don't have to be careful or conscious all the time of being Jewish. I am comfortable in this way. In Russia, I felt Jewish because I was not allowed to be Jewish. In prison, I felt like a human being because I was not treated as a human being. Here, I know I am a woman because I cannot be with my husband.

5

Ada Sereni

Enzo was a natural leader. He had a fantastic ability to find a common language with all men. The Arabs called him *Hawaja Chaim,* "Mister Life." Chaim was his Jewish name, Enzo his given name. He was part of Israel's hope for the future. This is why everyone was against his leading a group of parachutists into Nazi Europe. He was so obviously needed here. Ben Gurion even sent a message to Bari ordering him back.

He had suggested the secret mission as early as 1941, when news of the deportations and extermination camps first reached us. By 1942 we knew exactly what was going on. To an Israeli mind like his any delay was unbearable, but it was impossible to reach occupied Europe without British help.

Under British supervision, Enzo helped choose and then train with over thirty Jewish parachutists, but it took him over two years, until 1944, to convince the British to support the mission. He insisted on being dropped into Italy with the rest of the men. He was thirty-nine. I told him it was senseless, but he said he had to go.

Ostensibly he was to help British and American prisoners of war escape, but his real motive was to organize resistance, especially Jewish resistance. Resistance first, rescue if possible. He was already familiar with rescue work. Immediately before the parachute escapade, but unknown to the British, he had helped to evacuate thousands of Jews trapped in Iraq and bring them across the desert to Palestine. All this was illegal of course. Before this he was broadcasting propaganda on behalf of the allies to Italian prisoners in Egypt.

The last letter I received from Enzo was dated May 1944, from Bari, the headquarters of the parachutists. I think he knew he would not return.

Another man jumped with him, a Florentine, who was not Jewish. This man landed safely and reached Florence. Enzo, my husband, was supposed to be dropped behind the German lines, but he was parachuted directly on top of the German positions, forty miles from the prearranged point. He was captured immediately.

His brother claims it was a trick of British Intelligence, that it was done purposely. But there is no proof. Suspicion yes, but no proof. They knew he was a leader and therefore better dead than alive. I believe they had reason to fear him.

After the war the British army declared him missing. But to me it seemed impossible that a man of my husband's personality could vanish without a trace in a country that he knew from birth. So I decided to go to Italy myself to search for him.

The British did not help me. Why should they? As far as they were concerned he was missing in action, presumed dead. *Basta.* Anyway I didn't need their help. As soon as I got to Milan I took a Jeep and went on my own, and remember, I wore the uniform of a member of the British army attached to a Jewish unit. You couldn't get in any other way. The same underground office that sent my husband to Iraq arranged a cover for me as a welfare officer. I was running the canteen at one of the soldiers' clubs. The canteen was a blind.

By the time we opened the soldiers' club in Milan, the illegal ships with refugees were already leaving from Italy for Palestine, and I was co-opted to help. So I was already doing rescue work. Qualifications? I had no qualifications. I had been a housewife and during the war years while Enzo was away I was in charge of the jam factory on the kibbutz, making English marmalade for the British soldiers. I was so nervous, so full of tension, that I would never have believed that I would be in command of the whole operation in a year. But I think my husband would have approved. He would certainly have approved of my role in detaining the *Lino,* a ship carrying arms destined for Syria, until our people could sink her. Enzo, you see, had come to believe not only in rescue but also in active resistance. He had gone to tell his people the truth about the camps. He wanted to rally and lead the resistance, even though he was a pacifist.

Philosophically he was against war, but when what is happening is satanic, you have to choose between submission and self-defense. Enzo escaped from Paris only hours before the Nazis entered, and from then on he was driven, haunted by the plight of the Jews.

We came to Israel in 1927. Enzo was twenty-one. He was a pacifist, a doctor of philosophy. He wanted to be a pioneer, a Zionist in Zion, and give his life to this cause. We were distant relatives, both from comfortable homes. His was a highly cultured Roman family—his father was a physician to the king—and mine an *extremely* assimilated family. In my grandmother's house the word *Jew* was not permitted to be spoken in front of the servants and in my house it was never spoken at all. Both our fathers believed that the persecutions would never come again. But there was a difference.

Enzo's family looked down on mine. Although we had come to Italy from Spain when the Jews were driven out in 1492, to an established family like my husband's, which had been in Rome since the time of Julius Caesar, we were considered upstarts. And my family, for its part, would have nothing to do with him. Enzo was a socialist! In Rome he was forbidden to come to our house—for years we didn't exchange a word. But we had always been together in school. Day after day I followed him, and I think I have been in love with him, been under his spell, for as long as I can remember. Even at fifteen, he was convinced that *any* dictatorship—Mussolini or the Bolsheviks—would become anti-Semitic.

He was seventeen when he decided to come to Israel. I remember because we had already decided to marry. "All right," I said. "Let's go to Eretz Israel and be pioneers." He called himself an Eretz Israeli. We never spoke of this country as Palestine. Palestine means Philistine.

It was a great sorrow for my family that I took a Zionist husband and came to Israel to live in a tent. I had a newborn child when we arrived and Enzo became a worker in an orange grove.

Enzo would quote Hegel while he worked, and the

owner of the orange grove thought he was mad. "If you are a doctor of philosophy, what are you doing here?" Ben Gurion's people were stunned by this precocious young Italian who knew so much about European culture and history. He would read entire libraries. But he used to say, "I will never do anything really serious because I am a man divided." He was torn between his passion for living and his passion for literature. But in Israel he became an organizer in the workers' movement almost immediately, like Ben Gurion, and politics took over his life.

The following year, in 1928, the land that is now Givat Brenner was bought and we founded a kibbutz. He wanted a socialist society. We were a nucleus of twenty-eight people, and my two small babies were the only babies on the kibbutz. Enzo became the treasurer.

He was aware of the Arab question, maybe more than most of us. There were five Arab villages surrounding us in Givat Brenner. My husband loved people, so when there was a problem, the villagers came looking for Mister Chaim. One village had a terrible problem, a *mukhtar*, a head man, who oppressed them. They came to my husband and said, "Mister Chaim, we see that in Givat Brenner you have no *mukhtar*. Please tell us how we can get rid of our *mukhtar*." We were on very good terms with the Arabs until 1948, when what had to happen happened.

The last time Enzo was in Germany was in '34. He was arrested in a raid and—I can't vouch for this, but it sounds like him—when friends managed to arrange his release and came to get him, he didn't want to leave because he was deep in discussion with his jailers on the fundamental difference between Italian fascism and the Nazi party. He was a pacifist then and he remained a pacifist through the '36 to '39 riots when the Arabs threw bombs in the windows of the kibbutz. We were on guard for three years and he would not carry a gun. I know Golda says in her book that during the riots he would go alone and unarmed about the Arab villages at night, because he felt it was his duty to try and calm the Arab population, but I think Golda exaggerates. He wasn't unarmed, he just would not take a gun. He went with a whistle and a stick.

With the outbreak of the Second World War he went immediately to Europe. So many things that he did are unknown to me. There are many details I did not want to know, because under stress none of us knows how we will react to torture.

At school we had learned about Cromwell, and I always thought that English history stopped with Cromwell. But certainly, in the beginning, we had high hopes of the English.

I remember when the *Pan Crescent* sailed from Venice in 1947. She was a big ship, nearly seven thousand tons, one of the first big ships in my command, with a crew of twenty-three officers and enlisted men. The officers were afraid for their careers, afraid of this involvement with our underground.

I remember that British Intelligence came on board, and after they left a mine went off. They had attached an explosive device to the outside of the ship.

Did I expect this sabotage of them? Yes. They were

afraid of this big ship with its thousands of passengers reaching the shores of Israel. The *Exodus* affair was still strong in their minds.

We were lucky. The *Pan Crescent* was delayed at the last moment and the mine exploded while she was still in port. I know the intelligence people who went after us were unhappy because they felt that public opinion condemned them, but they followed their orders anyway. They were always on our heels.

Our ships had no flags, no documents. Their real names were canceled as soon as they departed so they couldn't enter any port. Only one of them was launched, because it was absolutely new. We found it at the shipbuilding yard and named it the *Enzo Sereni,* after my husband, when we got the news that he had been killed.

In 1945, as I was about to board the plane for Italy, I received a letter from a Dutch woman saying that she had met my husband in a camp in Germany. He had asked her to write to me if she got out of Dachau alive. That was the first concrete news I had, but I didn't believe it. Why Dachau? Enzo was wearing the uniform of a British soldier when he jumped and he spoke English. He should have been a prisoner of war. As soon as I got to Milan I interviewed survivors from Dachau. There was no trace of him. But I felt there was still hope, and I went to Klagenfurt on the Czech border where a refugee had said he had seen Enzo lying in a hospital. It was a false alarm and I lost the trail completely. Then one day I discovered from some Italians that he had been put in Mühldorf among the Italian political prisoners. He was in Mühldorf for some months. Then—I think now because he refused to take a British or American name and his papers said he was Jewish—he was suddenly transferred to Dachau, *senza coperte.* When a prisoner was sent away *senza coperte* ("without blankets"), it meant that he did not need blankets anymore. In Dachau we found his card, with the date of execution on it.

Afterward, I felt such despair. But I was in Italy for three years and I was never allowed to be alone with my thoughts. There was so much to be done—Italy was in chaos. Shops were empty. There were no cars, no trains. I was working with hundreds of soldiers. Our ships had to be found and provisioned. Refugees were pouring over the Alps and we had to transport them to a secret rendezvous and feed them. We moved them in trucks disguised as vegetables—sometimes with partisan help, sometimes not. Often we were discovered and sailings were canceled. Once, under the noses of the authorities, we drove a convoy of people to a health resort by the sea and staged a mock film of four hundred refugees boarding a ship, and then they sailed away. In this chaos the one and only organization was the army. We were army people, we provisioned the ships from British army stores. It was not very legal.

Thinking back to this game of cat and mouse sometimes I smile. There was at this time an English major stationed at the port in La Spezia who saw all our clandestine ships leaving and yet never understood that these were our ships. The British major was very British in that he didn't know a word of any other language. His secretary was an Italian working with us whom our commander had planted on him. Naturally when the major sent him on reconnaissance, the secretary "saw" nothing. This went on for months. The major got angry letters from Palestine where the ships were getting through. The secretary would translate them for the major and then afterward for us. In the restaurant we sat side by side—we at one table, the major and the secretary at another. The secretary would wink and we'd wink and the waiters who were in on it would also wink. And the British major of intelligence never understood.

What I remember most is how desperate these people were to reach Israel. The refugees were not ill—the ill ones were left behind—but they were still in shock and most of them had never seen the sea before. I think only desperate people would have undertaken this voyage. Our ships were terrible. They were new, but very small, and you cannot put nine hundred people on a six-hundred-ton ship and expect a comfortable ride to the promised land. Many ships—like the *Enzo Sereni,* like the *Exodus,* which was sent back to Germany, like the *Esmeralda*—were seized.

We could never have done it without the help of the Italians. Often the port authorities turned a blind eye, and the Italian people themselves were sympathetic. They knew about the camps. Now there are people who say it won't happen again—there are even Arabs who say it never happened at all—but thirty years ago it was a reality. Secondly, we could never have done it without young volunteers from the Palmach. They came from Israel and they took charge of the passengers. They were there to prevent panic and to resist arrest.

My daughter was the radio operator on board the *Esmeralda* when it was called to rescue another of our ships that was stranded off Corsica. About five hundred passengers were transferred to the *Esmeralda,* then it ran aground. The captain was an old Sicilian, a charming gentleman, but not very capable. He was lost in fog twice and then he collided with an ancient fort in Naples. Part of the fort collapsed. Off Calabria, the motor stopped functioning. Next the ship was escorted to Messina under arrest and held for twelve days. Finally it ran into a gale and was driven ashore off Crete. After a month it reached Israel, where the ship was seized and the passengers deported to Cyprus and interned. My daughter was taken ashore on a stretcher.

Did I know she was aboard? Of course I knew, I was the commander. But if I, her mother, had tried to stop her she would not have listened. But I did not try to stop her. It was clear to me that she had to go. This was our life and we were ready for it. It was her duty to go.

The first ships we sent reached Israel, but then, when the question of Cyprus came up, we knew that every ship would be seized. The *Enzo Sereni* had a charmed voyage. By mistake she was taken outside territorial waters—it was the British who broke the law this time—so after a court case the passengers were allowed to go free. But the British never made this mistake again. We knew we couldn't break the blockade, but it was not just a question of bringing these people; the ships were also a way of applying pressure. It was a political fight. We wanted to keep on sending these people until the British would grow tired and would leave this country. On May 14, 1948, they finally left this country. And then, because my job in Italy was done, I came home.

Although I have been here fifty years, it is still true that, just as in Italy I was a Jew, here I am an Italian. I loved

Italy, but to me Israel is an immense wonder, and from the day we started to build the kibbutz there was never any question of going back. When I see now how the country is green I always remember how it was when we landed. It was yellow. The country has changed color. And now my grandchildren and my great-grandchildren are here.

My husband used to speak of the ancientness of his people, and he came to Israel to be a Jew among Jews. I followed him for this reason. Anywhere else I am at the mercy of the government. It is very simple. *I want to be in a country where I can defend myself when I am attacked.* Even liberal governments change their song, can become anti-Semitic—liberal Germany became Hitler's Germany, liberal Italy became Fascist Italy, democratic France became Vichy France. And I think that when other countries try to weaken Israel, they are toying with their own destruction. You always hear about the six million Jews killed in the concentration camps, but another six million non-Jews *were also killed* in the concentration camps. And Spain is still paying for the Jews who were thrown out in 1492.

Anti-Semitism doesn't come down from the skies—it is always a sign. When Jews are attacked, it is always a sign that something is wrong in society. We are on the front line, we are the first targets, but after us come the others.

6

Yoram Krivine

We were finishing army service when the war started. I had two weeks to go and was looking forward to starting university. We were serving on the Golan Heights facing Syria, and the line was changed. "There they are," we were told by the man in charge of the post we relieved. He gave us a description. "There sits Division One, there is Division Two, here is Division Three, here is Division Four, and thank God when it starts I'll be somewhere else."

That was the first hint we had that anything might happen. That was on Tuesday. Friday afternoon we went into alert. Saturday lunchtime the planes came down on our post. I was quite surprised. No one had mentioned the word *war*. I didn't know there was a war until two o'clock the next morning when I turned on the radio. I couldn't get to a radio before then because we were shelled. We were shelled for twelve hours straight —on Yom Kippur. When the shells came down on the post it was very strange and frightening. There were eighteen of us. No one had ever fought in a war before. There was one officer, a year older than the others but a year younger than me. I was twenty-one.

In the beginning we were all in shock. We were sitting on the very front line. The reserves never got to us. We were right in the middle. The Syrians had already passed us. Their tanks ran right over us. It was a war of tanks. Then their guns passed us and they started building artillery and ambulance bases behind us. All we could do was sit in the trenches counting the tanks and try and tell our own artillery farther back where to go, what to do. Eventually, we had to sneak our way back.

The officer lost his fear first, then the sergeants. I had about eight soldiers under me and I was responsible for making them feel cool and relaxed. One of the soldiers was stuck in a post by himself and as a sergeant I was supposed to go and get him. I left the trench and I heard the terrible noise of a shell coming down. I jumped back. I had to keep doing this many times before I had the courage to go to the soldier.

We became very fatalistic at this point because we were running out of ammunition. We counted a hundred Syrian infantry trucks coming our way. "Evacuate us immediately or we're collecting stones to stop them," our commander said over the radio. Everyone in the bunker heard this. At this point people started mumbling and praying. The religious kids were praying. We knew about raiding and going forward, but not backward. When the order came we had one minute to leave the post. I left everything—documents, money, books, clothes. We went in a tank, actually a half-track. We all got into a half-track with the bodies of the dead and we just sneaked our way back—some luck. I remember that there were two tanks closing on us but for some reason they didn't fire. Our commander threw a hand grenade into the top of the nearest tank and it blew up. The other tank just ran away. But it was all too quick, it was a matter of hours. All the interesting things happened in the first twenty-four hours.

For example, on the evening of Yom Kippur I fasted. I'd never fasted before that day, but there was a religious boy in our unit and he talked us into it. He's what we call a *Gush Emunim.* Very strictly religious, but a bit too fanatic for my taste. To be religious in the army means you have to wake up half an hour early to pray; on the time breaks you have to pray and not rest. These minutes of rest are very important and to give them up you have to have strong mental powers, and this guy had them. "Come on," he said. "Come and pray for Yom Kippur. C'mon, do it once. What have you got to lose?" He played a bit on our feelings, and I said, "Okay, I'll fast this year." Nine of us fasted, two didn't. (We were eleven on the post at this stage.) The next day when the war began I had to break my first fast ever, and the only two people killed were the two who didn't fast.

My father isn't religious. He is totally unreligious like me, but when he knew I was on the front line, he wrote a letter without knowing if it would reach me. It came a week later. He said, "If you come out of this war alive, and if you wish, I am willing to go to synagogue every Saturday from now on." But I didn't insist on it, so he didn't have to go.

Many times I've asked myself, Why did I decide to fast? I haven't been able to find a good explanation.

You started thinking about the army at the age of fifteen. My images were mostly of raids, going across the border at night. Later we were taken on some raids. At sixteen you're thinking about choices—where will I go? Will I be a pilot? A paratrooper? At seventeen you're asking questions, very detailed questions. How tough is it? How many hours sleep a night? Do I obey an order if it seems wrong? Things like that. You get ideas from the kids coming back on leave. And then you're in it, and you can't get out of it. The first year in the army you talk only about the army.

My parents didn't come to Israel till 1950, so the whole pioneering thing, that special underground feeling of building the country, skipped them completely. I was born the year after they came from England. Schooling here is wild. No strict discipline, no barriers. Once a year we go for a trip and that week we drive our teachers out of their minds. The thing I remember is the informality. Corporal punishment? Never! Once a teacher in Tel Aviv slapped a kid in the face and he was taken to court. I mean, there is discipline—they used to throw kids out of classs all the time—but there's no fear.

Anyway, at seventeen I volunteered for the paratroopers. All my army friendships were formed at school. Everybody went in without exception. Not go into the army? It doesn't happen.

My whole class volunteered for combat units. We were an elite school, but we also had one class of kids from very bad homes—Moroccans, Tunisians, Iraqis, Egyptians, all the Oriental countries. We adopted a class of them and after four years we all finished as one lot. More than half the Oriental kids volunteered for combat fields. I served with some of them, and we were together nearly two years.

We say that a soldier is like soap. It means he does

everything exactly right, by the book. But it's not a compliment, because if you can sneak off, borrow a vehicle for a couple of hours without being caught, maybe bring back some Cokes, then you're *chevreman,* one of the guys. It means you're not afraid of the system.

After we were evacuated from the heights, we were taken to the Sea of Galilee, and we were just sitting, bathing and hearing news. And rumors. That's all we did for about a week. A third of the combat soldiers were out, nearly all the commanders were casualties, and one of the three groups in the battalion was practically wiped out. Then our colonel made a very big plea to the higher-ups to put us back into the war because he said we were under the trauma, the fear of running away. You can say "evacuated," but in fact we ran away—we didn't stay in our post. From Galilee we were taken to our base. There we got some reserves and built back the unit. There we waited.

My mother came back to Israel—she'd been in the States and couldn't get back—and I saw her for five minutes. She arrived at the base at seven o'clock and ten past seven we were on the buses going down to Egypt. The bridges across the Suez Canal were heavily shelled, and as soon as we came to the bridges we started getting back into fear.

I remember one soldier jumping off onto the bridge, trembling with fear and saying, "I don't want to pass, I don't want to pass the bridge." He was taken back.

We were brought into Africa, and moving on foot, we started cleaning an area. Suddenly I became a soldier.

Suddenly I started to function. We were supposed to clean an area on the west bank of the Canal and conquer it so as to enclose the Egyptian Third Army, which was sitting in the Sinai. We were the first across. We knew what to expect, we knew everything—that there were Egyptian soldiers, that they were in bunkers, that we were going inside these bunkers, that our air force had been over, that there were no Egyptian tanks. There were no tanks, but *lots* of Egyptian soldiers. In three days I remember we did what we had to do, and the soldiers were coming out and surrendering themselves all the time, even after the war ended. Coming out and coming out, from all sorts of holes and I don't know where. There were maybe a hundred of us but in three days we took two thousand prisoners.

We worked very slowly, according to all the training, and I remember thinking, It's a practice, it's like a practice. Only with live ammunition, so we were more careful—a bit worried, but that's all. We tried to get as many prisoners as possible. Some days afterward we were sleeping in a bunker when we heard a loud *rr-rrr* on the other side of the bunker. There were three Arabs sitting there. For three days they had been sleeping with us in the same bunker. We ran in and threw hand grenades; they surrendered. They were in every hole. You couldn't trace them all, although we looked and looked for them. For hours and hours we would be sitting on the vehicles in a state of alert, of almost moving, not knowing if at any moment we would be going back into war. We ate with our packs on. We used to open a can and eat the inside and fill it with fuel to make a stove to heat our coffee. We cooked our meals like that. There was nothing to burn.

Once the Egyptian soldiers started coming out, they didn't fight. They were terrified. I don't know what has been put in their heads, but they thought they would be slaughtered. All night long they chanted and wailed, "Sadat will die, Rabin will live," to draw pity on themselves. I remember whenever I gave a prisoner water or cigarettes he was astonished. I pitied him. You had to see the man in front of you, very weak and frightened, his eyes running, seeking any sign of hope. They were in shock. Maybe that is why one of them shot our guard. It happened the first night. We had a guard watching over two hundred prisoners. Suddenly a prisoner came forward with his hands up. It was night. He had a gun hidden. As he came forward he shouted, "I give in, I give in," and he just took the gun and shot our guard to death. Afterward we had huge arguments about it, about taking chances. It was very difficult because of this feeling of revenge. Revenge plays a big role, and how do you neutralize this feeling of revenge when one of your best friends is killed next to you like that?

We talked about it all the time—the value of life. We talked about the face of the country, how it should be, who should lead us. We tried to analyze a few people in our unit who ran away: why did they do that? One of the commanders came up and asked: Would we be happy to fight again? No one said yes. No one wanted another war. The anti-war feeling was very strong.

The elections took place while we were still in Africa and we voted from there. The soldiers from the combat units voted very left, very pacifist. I have an English cousin who thinks we are very right wing or fascist, and when he came to Israel we argued about it. I told him that among my friends we are much more leftist than rightist. It was hard for him to understand. Between 1947 and 1967, and even up to 1973, Israel was much more fascist than it is today. I mean the army had more control. Israel has a very strong army, a very big army, a very intruding army, but it is not a fascist country. People are very much aware of their civil rights, so that although the army is strong, the citizenship is also strong. I was brought up on that. They used to just take a general and give him a top job, but now there is a rule and that can't be done anymore.

In Africa we would sit around bonfires and talk all night, and I saw that people had become grown up. Especially my kids—I saw it in my soldiers. Much of the power, the strength to be courageous, comes from within the group, the family idea. Like the fasting I mentioned. It was easy to fast that time because we were together in a group. The idea is in the framework and the sharing of responsibility. The commanders inspired this. And I never had the feeling I'd be neglected.

I remember when we captured the Canal. We were clearing a trench and suddenly we were split up—the commander without warning took everyone back, leaving me and three others there alone. We had to do some fighting. They were gone and we were alone in an enemy area, but I never had the feeling that I would be forgotten. Five, six hours later they came and called us back. That's why immediately after the war began I was sent to that soldier who was cut off. The fact that I came to the soldier, *during the shelling,* when he was cut off and scared to bits, made him feel confident. I brought him to the others, and he felt part of the family again.

People say that war brutalizes. I've read it, I've heard

it. But it can also humanize. I lost three friends in that war, close friends. But now, if it happens again, if one of them was killed, say in a helicopter crash, I would overcome it quicker. I wouldn't carry it with me. You learn to treat death as less extreme—it shouldn't break the whole order of life. On the other hand, you have to visit the families. It's an obligation everyone feels. Three times a week I visit one of the girls whose husband was killed. She lost a brother and two husbands in three wars, a terrible story. You can't be too rough or arrogant, because these people are really damaged. You cannot stand indifferent to that, it's like an obligation to help a friend in fear. You have to go. I mean, nobody *likes* coming into a moaning home, especially a young kid with only twenty-four hours leave. I remember soldiers coming out of seven, eight weeks of not being at home. First they went home to their parents and then they went immediately to each family. That's the way you do it on a leave of twenty-four or forty-eight hours. Nobody tells you to do it. It's in the atmosphere, the framework—and there's no need to talk about it. Only in literature do they talk about it.

For a long time afterward I was having depressions—tensions, stomach trouble. The depressions were mostly nightmares. I kept seeing soldiers around me, coming out from holes. The nightmares began there on the spot; you saw so many people killed. Friends, people you knew. And the nightmares returned when I visited the families.

I served another six months after the war, sitting in Africa and Sinai, then because of the tensions I just had to get out. I went abroad and stayed with my cousins. I'd missed the opening of university anyway. I came to

England and I was very relaxed. Very depressed maybe, but very relaxed. I came with three friends, and my English cousins said we were too serious—too serious, and too responsible. I don't know.

I met a lot of English kids, fine. We had lots in common. What do I have in common with someone my own age in England? I think—everything.

Listen, we can talk about politics, sports, girls, everything. Yet maybe the English do treat us as if we were special creatures. I was in Butlin's. We were four Israeli sabras in Butlin's holiday camp—my aunt treated us— and the boys there, typically English, middle and working class, couldn't believe that we were Israelis. And the girls: I would invite one to dance and after a bit she'd say, "Where are you from?" When I said Israel, she'd say, "Go on!" and just leave me. They thought we were kidding them and they didn't like it. Twice it happened to me. I felt very strange.

I love England. We have a big family there, lots of relatives. I've been there a lot on visits, and my parents also slipped things into my personality by this back- door approach they have. After all, I just missed being born in England. So it was natural to me, easy. But I didn't feel like an English boy. Even though I had an English passport, I felt Israeli, sabra. And in England, without saying one word, we recognize each other—we come up to each other. You know if someone is Israeli. It's as if there is a kind of secret language.

There's a special look—I can't explain it. Agriculture look, maybe. Special walk and special dress, special shoes and carelessness. There's a flying jacket, an army jacket that everyone wears, and different jeans, working jeans. "He's Israeli." See him in the road, nothing bothers him.

In England I was very relaxed and my stomach troubles went away. It was so much easier after Israel. But somehow it was another vision. I had difficulty being part of it. In Israel we have a quarter in Jerusalem, Mea Shearim, for very religious people, very kosher. It's a small ghetto inside the country. And although I find it interesting and I like going there, the people of Mea Shearim are very strange to me. They belong to another world. It's a museum. In some ways I saw England like that: not as a place to compare with Israel but as something pleasant to look at. Everything quiet. A pleasant picture gallery to walk through.

People say that life is more real here. Jewish visitors from the Diaspora say it all the time. But it's not. It's just different. This is why I'm against separating religion from this country, separating religion and the state. Religion makes the difference. Personally I am not religious, but I don't think there's any contradiction. I'm Jewish, that's the fact of life. And I believe the country should be Jewish, has to be Jewish. Losing the religion makes it like any other country, like England or America. So why live here, take risks, go to war? If there is no meaning, if it's just another state? Why not live in Chicago? I think if you separate religion from the state you empty the whole country of its values and its Jewish identity. Here we are fighting with the Arabs because we are

Jewish, not because we are American. It has nothing to do with how I feel about religion. I just think it's the right idea for the country. This is the reason I stay? This is *the only reason* I stay. Take my father. Actually my father is the only member of a huge family who came to Israel. In many ways he is an example of what the others should have done, but didn't. He has a very powerful standing in the family only because he came here to live.

I don't want to live somewhere I'm worried about wearing the Star of David. When I went abroad people warned me about speaking Hebrew, about wearing the Magen David. And I remember being in Germany at a train station surrounded by Arabs and not speaking Hebrew. But after thinking to myself, What the hell am I afraid of? I started talking Hebrew freely and wearing Israeli T-shirts all over the place. Maybe the war helped liberate me. I don't know that I would have done this if I hadn't been in the war.

The fact that I experienced the war gives me status, a say in the political future of the country. I feel I'm needed. I didn't fight to liberate places, I never felt that Egypt was my land. The Tomb of Rachel, the holy places of Judea—they don't mean a thing to me. I don't see why Jews want to settle there. What's the big idea? I fought because of the feeling I'm needed, that I'm giving birth to the country, that without my help all the work would probably have to be done from the beginning all over again. I don't think I had this strong feeling before the war.

I'm very frightened of war. Another war.

My father would like me to be a politician, but that is one of the things I can't see. This country is so dynamic and changing that I can't see more than a year or two in front, into the future. I'm twenty-four. I haven't finished university yet. All I know is that in ten years time I will still be here and a part of what is happening. Maybe I'll be having a family, doing my time in the reserves, and settling down with a family. That's what I'd like. I can't see myself educating my sons into the army, but who knows.

This place was supposed to be a refuge. That is what the old people wanted. That was the Zionist dream: a place that will be safe for our children. I don't feel the way they felt, I mean I already feel differently because I'm here. A house that is quiet and safe for the kids? Logically, when I try to analyze the situation, it seems hopeless. Not logically, it seems hopeful.

How can I present it right? There's a famous quote in the Bible: *Ish tahat gafno ve tahat te'enato* ("Everyone under his vine and under his fig tree sitting quietly and happily"). It seems far, far away. It seems like Utopia. I can't get into those shoes at all.

7

Nurit Shiloh

The day after they took Jerusalem we went into the streets. That Thursday of 1967 was the first day that we could go into the streets. What a day! We went to my aunt to buy flowers. I sent flowers to everyone I knew, everyone I could think of. We went to the banks, not to get money, but to *donate* money—to buy government bonds; everyone did that. We have already given a fixed amount from our salary to buy bonds, but this day we buy twice. Buy twice, buy thrice, it doesn't matter.

When I was sending the flowers I met a girl friend from school. I said shalom and she said, "I hope they're all right." That was all. She went on down the street. It was a sunny day. Later we understood that her husband was killed in the Old City. We weren't allowed in there. Only the children, the soldiers who were fighting, were allowed in the Old City.

Not all the shops were open, because some people didn't know whether or not to open. There was a soldier sitting on the step outside the shop. He looked terribly tired, as if he hadn't slept for six days. He was just sitting there. He had a gun. He looked so funny, though not at all sad. Suddenly the door opened and the shopkeeper saw him there. "Come in, come in. Why sleep there?" she said. "Come and eat, drink something. Everything, everything is for you. You deserve everything in the world." And he said, "You think we deserve everything in the world, but you never saw what I saw in the war. So just leave me alone." He was very young.

We *had* seen the fighting. The night they took Jerusalem we went up to the roof. Everyone knew that it was happening. The noise. The Dormition Abbey was burning. You could see every shell in the night because of the lights. And when we were sure it was ours we cheered. I said to my husband that it seemed as though the walls of the building shook from our happiness. But our son couldn't understand it. Like all our children, Talmi got a very humane education—fighting, all this, is not something that they teach. So Talmi shouted, I remember this so clearly, he just shouted at us. He was in tears.

Although it was literally next door, until that night we had been shut out of the Old City. Five hundred yards away was a concrete dividing wall, and for twenty years we hadn't known what was going on behind it. I hadn't ever been there, yet I knew it. I knew it from my childhood, from the Bible, from our history. I don't know how it is in your country, but to us, when we study history, it's like an operation on our bodies. So I knew it again and again, from face to face and from one level to another, as if it's a part of me. I knew the stones, although I had never been there.

Thursday evening my father came from Tel Aviv with his car. I don't know how he got here, because the roads weren't open. I think he found a way along the railway tracks. "Come on," he said. "I want to go to the Old City." Dudu, my husband, said, "You're crazy, it's impossible. The war's still on." Never mind, my father wanted to see.

Of course it was impossible! Everything was blocked. There were no shops open, not one shop. But there was a tank, an Israeli tank that had rolled down a hill. Three people had died in the tank, and their bodies were still there. We came through the Mandelbaum Gate, and Dudu produced a paper from the Foreign Office—actually it was worthless—and Father said he knew the way. Which way? "To the *kotel,* to the Wall." But then we saw that he didn't know the way, that everything had changed. We left the car and went through the Lion's Gate, where the soldiers had gone in. Actually an Arab showed us the way. When we arrived near the Jewish Quarter, the houses were so crowded, very different from how it is now. Everything was so tiny there within the walls. We didn't know if people lived in these rooms or if they were only yards. Funny way of living, I thought. The Wall was within. The Arabs were placid, calm, as if nothing had happened. We saw a little girl sweeping a courtyard. I said to Dudu, "She is much older than she looks. It's malnutrition." She is the one who guided us to the Wall. "Yes, you can go on. In there," she said. Of course, the Wall was hidden. We passed through steps and stairs and yards. It was as if there was no war. Then all of a sudden we arrived.

It wasn't dark yet. We couldn't hear any noises at all, although many people were there, mostly army people. Everyone was weeping but in a very discreet way, very privately. Everyone kept to himself. We are not a quiet people—not quiet at all. But then it was quiet. People were praying but you couldn't hear them.

I stood aside. I thought that because I was wearing slacks I should stay aside. Actually that was an excuse; I wanted to stay aside. I didn't want to go near it. I didn't know what to do, how to confront the thing or how to relate to it.

It wasn't *familiar,* it was more than familiar. After two thousand years the impossible became possible. It wasn't open to the public—we just sneaked in. To live a moment like that, a simple moment. You feel at that moment that you are living history. And the soldiers felt it, too. They had been fighting of course. This is why they cried. And they—all of a sudden it comes back to them: This Wall is not just a wall. And there was a lot of pain there.

A stranger will not understand this.

We came back the same way, but not in the same way. Once we were trapped in a minefield. We got out and then my father said he wanted to see Mount Scopus, where the university is. That, too, had been cut off. On the way to Mount Scopus, again I was aware of how calm the Arabs were. There was a very old couple, and I am sure they didn't even know who was fighting and what for, who won or who lost. They were completely detached. They were dressed like fellahin and living in a tiny thing made not of mud but of stones collected one on top of the other. That was outside of the Wall. On the main street, on the main roads where the fighting was, there were jumbles of stones. The soldiers collected the stones and used them to mark the places where people were killed. They wrote the names of the dead on the stones with something that looked like blood, although I don't think it was blood.

We saw these markers on every corner. And then I couldn't bear it any more. I said to my father, "Look, what are we doing? We are touring the place!" I was so angry at us. I broke down and cried, and we came home.

As a girl my mother was taken to the Old City by Arab friends. She had to dress up like an Arab and go in disguise. The Wall meant everything to her. Was she religious? No, no more than I, but her people were religious. They came to Jerusalem from Spain two hundred fifty years ago. They came to die, to be buried here, the same as my father's people. But she was not religious. So why did she go to the Wall? Why now when I walk in the Old City does the stone mean so much to me? Why do I walk in its shadow? Why do I touch it? Why did the children, the eighteen-year-old soldiers who were also not religious, why did they cry when they came to the Wall? Why was it so spontaneous? It is one of the mysteries that this city and this country hold. My husband tells a story of a friend of his who was an army commander and fought in the Old City during the war. He was told, "Take the direction of the Wall." Now he was born in the Old City, not by the Wall but somewhere in the Jewish Quarter. His house was there. And he said, "To hell with the orders. I'm not interested in the Wall, I'm going to my house." He left the unit—he was the commander—and he went home, to see his house. For him it was a birthplace, and it's the same for me. It's

more than the holiness of the Wall. Jerusalem—it's a
dream, you are walking in a dream.

It's like a sickness. This is what the doctors said to me.
But after three weeks of examinations and tests, they
finally said, "There is nothing wrong with you." At first
they thought I had a thyroid problem. One doctor was
so sure that what was wrong with me was something
physical that he tried to force the results of tests to fit
his diagnosis. But after three weeks of tests he admitted
he had made a mistake. He said, "There is nothing
wrong with you except that you belong here. You
should never leave this place." We had been sent to
Burma in the early sixties. It was Dudu's first posting
with the Foreign Office, and it was the first time I had
been away. I was unhappy in Burma. I lost weight. Then
the dreams began. All the dreams of Jerusalem begin in
Burma. I had said nothing to the doctor about my dreams
or why I'd suddenly flown back. We had orders to go
from Burma to Japan. We had the tickets. But then, with
my own money, I bought new tickets for Talmi and
myself and we flew back to Jerusalem to beg them not
to send us to Japan. Then Dudu came. The second day
I was here I collapsed and was put into a hospital. That
was when they did all those tests and found out it was
just homesickness.

Being homesick to me is not being homesick for any
person—it's not for people. It is being homesick for
Jerusalem. For me, Jerusalem is Israel.

In the end we went to Japan. And the dreams went on,
they never ceased. In one dream I am running up Ben

Yehuda Street, running up the hills as if there is no time, *swifting.* Absorbing as much as possible as quickly as possible. And the swifting—a terrible noise, running like the wind—the swifting takes you and you can't resist. And always returning to places that I know. Touching the stones which are very cold stones, because it is night —the daytime I don't like anyway. Quickly I come to the marketplace, but still I can't stop. Then I run to the house, the house of my childhood.

I inherited this sickness from my father, who had it much worse than I did. Mine wasn't really sickness, but *his was.* When he was studying engineering in France he got so homesick for Jerusalem that he went to pieces. He got over it eventually, but he had to come back to Jerusalem first before he could finish his studies.

He was two when his people brought him here from Hungary. Those who didn't come were of course killed in the Holocaust. His people came here to die, to be buried on the Mount of Olives.

I didn't leave Jerusalem until I was married. Before that I had refused to go four times. Like Dudu, I was also at the Foreign Office and had a wonderful job as a minister's secretary. According to tradition, the secretaries from that office got the best jobs in the world. Right away they offered me London. I remember how mad my father was with me for refusing. Then they said Paris. After that anywhere in the United States. I gave in only when I married Dudu, but then it was his career and I didn't have much choice. But I remember when he told me he was being posted that I said to him, "We're doomed."

After we came back from the Far East there were more

offers, more posts—Africa, Dar es Salaam, Cambodia— but I woudn't leave Jerusalem. We had six years, '64, '65, '66, '67— we were so lucky to be here during the war— then '68 and '69. We kept saying, "Choose someone else," and it worked for six glorious years. Until we had to go to Australia.

In Australia the dreams began again. I was so afraid of those dreams—running the streets, the hills, to the market place, then to the house. Into that house.

It was a beautiful house, built by the English for the United Nations commission when they had to decide on the partition of Palestine in 1947. It had walls of stone and inner courtyards—lots of families living there—and a proper terrace. I came there with my parents because the Arab house we were living in before was bombed by the Haganah, by our people. Outside there was a field, which to me, a child, seemed huge. To get to school I had to cross the field. It was full of thorns. I remember the thorns cutting my legs and the soil that was cracked because of the heat. And the ants. When I was tired I would sit in the field to rest and watch the ants climb up my legs. Then I would brush them off and I would go home. But not in 1948. In 1948, when we first came there, we couldn't leave the house. We couldn't go out the front door because the War of Independence was on and there were shots all the time.

Fifty yards away was the Katamon front, the Arab barracks. They shot from there. You know what is fifty yards? Nothing at all. The Arabs were on top of the hill, we were down below. They shot all the time. We got used to it. The young people were away fighting— maybe once a week they would come for a night to see how we were. My father organized the resistance. Once he fired a bullet that wasn't considered absolutely necessary and there was such a fuss. But it was easy to fool the Arabs, they were such fools. My father placed life-size cardboard cutouts on the roof. Also sandbags, as many as possible. It was a large roof. When he had time he went on the roof and, going from one sandbag to another, answered the fire. Usually there was only him on the roof, but sometimes my mother would go to help shoot. This is how we survived. The Arabs were so sure that we were many more people. We could pass from one place to another only when the house itself protected us. As a child of nine years old, I knew exactly how to hide, not just behind the building but later on when I left the building and it couldn't shelter me any more, I knew exactly how the curves of the ground went and whether or not they could see me. You think it was silly to stay? It was not silly, it was very clever. Because if we had left, they would have had the house. We *could* have left, but we didn't want to. It's a very sacred principle: it's very easy to leave a house, but then you have to take it back.

Once men came during the night, and I overheard these rumors that children were not supposed to hear, that thousands and thousands of Arabs were sweeping against us. We had to leave the apartment and go down by rope—we always went down with a rope—to the one below, which had a kind of basement. We slept there. I felt like I was in a cave. I was terribly afraid of what they were saying. I remember sleeping with my hand pressed against the wall so it wouldn't fall on me.

My dreams in Australia, in Canberra, were not about

the '48 war. They were about another war that I missed. Do you know what it means that there was a war and I was not here? It means that somebody else did the fighting. We were not here and we will never get over it.

In Canberra, Dudu used to get up very early and turn on the radio. This is why I remember the dream, because if it hadn't been for the news and Dudu opening the radio, I would have forgotten it. It begins again with whispering. People are whispering and they don't want me to hear. Little by little I understand that something is going on in my house. I'm in Australia. I see my bathroom in Jerusalem and there are worms walking on the walls, not many, very few. But it is serious, it's a very serious situation because *worms are in my house.* Next to the bathroom is a closet containing my good clothes. And my mother is there and she is taking out every garment to see if it is infected. If the worms have touched it, she puts it aside. She does this in a very serious manner. Now the whisper is louder. "I'm going home," I say, "I have to go." I'm walking from Australia. I'm in the field now, this huge field, and I have to cross it in the heat. I hate the summer and I hate the heat, but I *have* to cross it.

A woman has come. The moment I leave Australia, a woman comes with a tray containing food. "Here," she says. "You have a long way to go." But I ignore her and walk on. Why take a tray with me? The woman comes again with the tray. "You will need it," she says. She is so insistent that in the end I take the tray, knowing that I shouldn't. Now I am with the tray of food crossing the field and I'm tired, terribly tired. The thorns are cutting my legs and I can't go on. I have to rest. I say to myself, "I am going to sit down," just like when I was a child. I sit down with the tray of food on my lap. The food is arranged in a very attractive manner and I look at it and think, "Just a bit. I'll eat just a little bit." As I do this I feel some of those ants crawling up my legs. I brush them down. "Can't I sit down for one second without those things bothering me!" I laugh and brush them down. I go on eating. But now they're coming up, up and up, and it's more serious. Suddenly I jump. Everything is flying and I'm running like mad into the house. As I enter it, I see two men, strangers, dressed in white, with their backs to me. "I'm here, I've arrived," I say. "But what about these ants!" The two men are absorbed in what they are doing; they barely notice me. "Oh, all right," they say. "Just go in there and wash them down." I go into the bathroom and at first there is very little water, only drops. But now, ah, the relief, because they're coming down. They're coming down. . . .

I told Dudu what it meant as soon as I woke up. It was there on the news on the radio. The home is of course Israel and the worms represent death. In sleep the mind and the brain work in symbols, but I didn't know it then. People are dying and I should be there, but instead my mother is there, someone on whom I can rely. She is taking the garments—the bodies—and separating the living from the dead. And others are helping, they are treating the dead. Everything is under control.

The tray is the most important thing. I'm going home. I'm in a hurry, yet the tray is something I have to take with me. The tray is connected to Yom Kippur, the Day of Atonement. In 1973 we were attacked on Yom Kippur, at the very moment when the country was settling down to the traditional feast. The tray of food is Yom Kippur itself and it's Judaism as I see it—something that I cannot leave behind. I have to carry it, even if it is in my own blood, in my own bloodstream. It is this that I have to take with me, my being Jewish.

What's interesting is that in the dream I took the tray exactly as I take Judaism. I take it but it's not important. I take it just because I was given it. I didn't throw the tray away, I did carry it as much as I could. But it's *such* a nuisance to me. And then, the one second that I sat down to rest, the one second that this country sat down to rest and enjoy the feast of Yom Kippur—because this country cannot be on the alert all the time—then the ants started to crawl. But the ants were a joke, because the Arabs at that time were a joke to me. Little bit of attack here, little bit of attack there. They're like the ants of my childhood. Brush them down, down and away. But then, when they came up above my lap, then I jumped like this country jumped! You know that the soldiers in '73 went into battle wearing slippers? They had no time to change.

But the main thing was that the men in white, the doctors, were treating the dead. That was the main thing, taking care of the tragedy.

I think the explanation is obvious. When I awoke, I said to Dudu, "For God's sake, can dreams be *so clear*?"

Since we came back from Australia people are not the same. Not like they were in '67. We're missing something.

I'm talking about values.

Take Stella, the woman on the next landing. Her family owns the biggest bakery in Jerusalem. In '67 the first thing she and her husband did, immediately after the Old City was taken, was to fill the bread vans with bread and distribute it from door to door because they thought the Arabs were starving. The same with milk for the children. People thought of these things then.

You think I'm expecting too much of a people? It was a crisis and in a crisis you respond. But I still expect— I expect it of this people and I expect it of my city. That's why I say Jerusalem is more than a place. It's not Canberra. Canberra—oh beautiful, perfect—Canberra is a place to live in. Jerusalem is not just for living. Jerusalem is *being*.

Everything that happened here up to '67 had another dimension and it wasn't even logical. Actually it was against logic and if it existed in people at all, this other dimension, it was in spite of logic. We needed it then and we had it and I hope we still have it. But somehow it's hidden. I'm talking about normal human things. I'm talking about the feeling of "Well, everything's all right. Now we can behave like everyone else in the world." We can't.

Normal is not right for us. Bribes, corruption—this is not a way for us. It's not because we want to be better, but because in our case it does not work.

I told you of Talmi's reaction in '67. It was also part of that dimension people had. Talmi wasn't just angry with us, he didn't just shout. He made a speech. He said, "Why are you so happy people are killed there?" He didn't mean the Israelis, he meant the other side. "You tell me that you are victorious, then there must be the other side which is *not* victorious! So why are you so happy?" He was six years old and he made this speech, then went to sleep for twenty-four hours.

So this was part of the education he had at that time in Jerusalem. I, too, because I went to the same school. Not hate, but love. We were fed on love. If someone fell down in the street not one but a dozen people would rush to pick him up. I'm not exaggerating, that was the feeling! Despite the wars, despite the shortages, despite the siege. At that time this country was only nine miles across, it was a joke. But 1967 was the culmination. Maybe it's the very ancient concept of pride that kills everything. That pride is the enemy of the soul. Because it was pride in '67. It was a pride that we deserved, because the Six Day War was so fantastic, so magnificent. And then when we were proud we *became* proud, and that was the beginning of the fall.

Read the Bible, the Old Testament. It's the same people, I can see it today! It's as if nothing has changed. It's the people of extremes—either *this,* or *that. Normal* is not a word in our dictionary. And if we think we're being normal today, we're kidding ourselves. This is not normal. It's worse than normal.

We have to live on values. It was said so many times, *Lo bechail ve-lo bechoach ki im beruchi amar hashem tsevaot.* ("Not by might nor by power but my spirit"). There is no way out of this. Strength is spiritual. So God forbid if we forget that.

If we forget that, we don't exist. It happened in the past. So take it symbolically. God will punish or not punish, it doesn't matter, this will be the end. And the pride, it's again in the prophets. I'm not religious, there is no religious aspect to it. Maybe we really deserved the pride in '67. We felt that God was there to do it, to help. Just for a second, you know? So there was great joy. But then the petty things, the petty people who thought, "They're under us, the Arabs," the feeling that we're better. So maybe the pride was what started this curse. Prophets are of course extreme people because they feel strongly about these things, but the prophets said, "We are the love or the beloved of God." This was how they put it. God has chosen us and that was so clear. And look what we're doing. Of course there's no *normal* if God chose it. But what now? Why can't we become normal? And yet this is a law. It's a law that you can't change. We cannot afford to be as other nations are.

Being here is half the job. Oh, I know people are leaving Israel all the time for America, for a "better economic future." They're crazy. They don't know anything better. They have no brains. Being here is still a privilege, despite what I have said, despite our being so tired and so horrible to one another. We're tired because we make hell for one another. Do you know why the people in Japan are so polite? Why so much energy goes into manners? Because otherwise they would have killed one another—there are so many of them. Here we have no manners. It's hell. But to be here is still the greatest privilege on earth.

There's a price, too. Miriam came home from school the other day, right after Passover. It was the memorial day of the Holocaust and the teachers told her about

Anne Frank and showed a film. Miriam said, "You know, Mother, that was worse than when we were slaves in Egypt." Miriam is only seven years old.

They say here that we have to *know.* When they say this to me, I shout. I say, "I'm not going to tell my children in a way that will shock them like this!" It will shock them one day, I know. It happened to me. As a child I used to bring books home from the library, but if I had a book about the Holocaust I couldn't read it. I wouldn't. The same when I was a teen-ager. It wasn't until we were in Burma in 1961 and those reports from the Eichmann trial started coming in that it caught me. Suddenly I couldn't stop reading about it.

The reports were daily dispatches coming into the embassy. They came in bundles, every word that was said at the trial. People fainted in court, here in Jerusalem. People who were there and heard those words that I read, fainted. I was pregnant with Talmi. And when I gave birth, when I was on that table in the act of giving birth, I couldn't think of anything but the trial. I was *there.* Because there was a scene they described at the trial about a woman in one of the camps giving birth . . . of course they killed it, they killed the child immediately. And the German officers who witnessed the murder found it a very interesting experience to watch. So while Talmi was being born I was there.

It catches up with you. It catches up with you like the tray in my dreams. Maybe the people here are right when they say we have to know.

I don't know what Talmi knows, how much he is aware of. He hasn't faced it yet. Actually the same day that Miriam was told about Anne Frank, Talmi's class was taken to Yad Vashem, the memorial to the six million who died in the Holocaust. Talmi wasn't feeling well that day so he didn't go. He escaped it, and he should have gone. As it happens, I was quite pleased that he escaped.

Talmi is fifteen. I don't know how he will serve in the army. You might say that now he has a problem. Sometimes when I look at him I see that scene of the soldier in the street, sitting on the step in front of the shop. Talmi has changed a lot since '67, since "the war of the children," as I called it. But actually they weren't all children in that war—that war, the '67 war, was the war of the professors and the doctors. Half of those who fought had a degree from somewhere. It was the next war, the '73 war, that was really the war of the children. I don't know how Talmi would have reacted if we had been here for that.

8

Olivia Zetler

I left alone—not knowing if I would come back. Left Aaron, left the children. I went to London.

Most of my friends and family in England thought it very strange that I was living in Israel anyway. I left feeling very bitter, very hostile. I left feeling I didn't want to see another Israeli or hear another Hebrew word as long as I lived. The language *infuriated* me. People would talk to you in English, oh yes, but only for the first few months. After that they didn't make the effort. How could I belong? We'd go to a party and there would be a whole group of people who were together at university in Jerusalem from '37 to '42—elites. Or not even elites, just a strong feeling of belonging because they had been on this kibbutz together, in the Palmach together, in Jerusalem in the old days together—like Aaron, my husband. I didn't have the involvement. On the other hand, when we first arrived a year after the war, everyone was leaving, wanting to get out and not come back because of the war and the aftermath. All round me was this feeling of despair and a terrible compulsion to get out. How do I have a chance, I thought, when these

107

people who belong here, who were reared here, don't want to live here anymore?

London was *so good.* This marvelous euphoric feeling —of reading everything and understanding everything that went on in the streets and in the buses and in the shops. But still, after a few days I found myself looking in the papers for little things like "Israeli elections," "Rabin says . . . ," you know. I began to wonder what was going on. People kept saying to me, "How was it?" My generation had never been through an actual war. They wanted to know, and I had to try and explain. I wasn't allowed to get away from it. I was sucked in? Sucked back, you mean.

I was back in three weeks.

Walking away hadn't solved anything. The personal crisis in my marriage which had been brought to a head by living in Israel, that remained. I still resented living in a place that was not primarily of my own choosing. The only reason we were here was because Aaron had come home. Now I had to decide whether I was going to divorce my husband or remain married to him and stay in Israel.

Now the whole question of Jewishness, of my becoming Jewish, came up. I thought that if I became Jewish it would give me the commitment I needed to stay. Then, when I made an offer to convert, when I was already taking instruction, the rabbi said, "They can come and check to see if you are both keeping Shabbat." If you convert, the most important thing is that you observe the Sabbath. That means no driving, no teaching, no anything. I came home and said to Aaron, "Look, you're expected to keep it too, mate. Not only me." And he responded, "They're going to tell *me* how to be Jewish!" So he wasn't very helpful.

I have lived all my life uncommitted. Yet when we arrived in Israel, apparently "Jewish" was written on my identity card. But I didn't realize it because I don't speak the language. I'm illiterate, you see. I can't read Hebrew.

Aaron says I have this psychological problem that I need to say I am *not* something, that I have a pathological thing about not belonging. Maybe it's my Indian blood.

In Pakistan, where I was born, we used the word *Jew* to mean the people who killed Jesus Christ. My father was in the Indian Civil Service and I was boarding at a convent school. We were domiciled British. When we moved to Calcutta in 1947 there was a community of Sephardim, Baghdadi Jews from Iraq. We lived in the top half of a huge Indian-Jewish house that belonged to an actress. I met these black Jews. That was my first contact with Jews of any kind. Later in England I discovered Jews as people, but in India, until we came to Calcutta, I had never thought of them in that way at all. The Indian Jews were more European than Jewish, they were like us—"domiciled Europeans." And then there were Europeans and then there were Indians. These Jews were the black Jews of Cochin. I didn't know anything about them except that suddenly, in 1948, a group of them went to Israel. And the whole lot, practically the whole lot, returned. They told terrible stories about Israel, about the conditions and primitive people. These Cochin Jews were merchants, well-off and spoiled. They came to Israel out of curiosity and were not able to cope at all.

I was twenty-one before I knew about the word *anti-Semitism.* I just hadn't heard about it. Un-be-lievable! There was no anti-Semitism in India. I was aware of color prejudice, I was aware of the caste system, I was very much aware of social distinctions, but not anti-Semitism.

In England I found out about it from the inside. I was working for a Jewish publisher, a crazy Polish guy— totally self-made man. And he said to me—marvelous phrase—"You know, Olivia, for a *shiksah* you're a hell of a nice girl. Best thing we can do is marry you off to a nice Yiddishe boy."

Then I met Aaron. He was an Israeli. But you know I didn't even know that Israeli was necessarily Jewish. I met him as Aaron, a philosopher. An Israeli and an intellectual. He was a very strange creature to Henry, the man I worked for. Henry didn't really speak to me after I'd decided to leave him and marry Aaron. At first he was furious because he'd lost the best secretary he'd ever had. Then—it was very strange. I said, "Well, here you are, here's your nice Yiddishe boy." And Henry said, "He's not a Yiddishe boy. He's a bloody Israeli!"

Through Henry I'd already met a couple of nice Jewish boys, very nondescript and terribly polite. I suppose they considered it a little daring to go out with a non-Jew. I invited them home but I noticed they didn't introduce me to their mothers. Gradually, I began to understand. My family was Catholic. I thought, "Well, if I convert it should be all right." But it wasn't quite like that either, as it turned out.

In England there was a strange sort of veiled anti-Semitism. "Oh these rich Jews, they've taken over the place," English friends would say. *Idiotic* remarks like that. Then I began to understand the exclusivity of the Jews themselves. So here was a parallel with what I'd had in India—lumping people together because they were born a this or a that, this was what I had come to England to get away from.

But the clannishness struck me only after I was married. Aaron had just finished Oxford and was taking his first teaching job in Dublin when I met him. I knew nothing about him except that he was born in Hungary and all his family barring one or two cousins was killed in the war, in the camps. I was actually engaged to somebody else—I was supposed to marry somebody in India. I told Aaron that I didn't know him very well and didn't want to get married anyway. "Marriage or nothing," Aaron said. And that was it.

We had a civil ceremony in the only registry office there was in Dublin. We were both half drunk or I don't think we would have gone through with it.

It was all very quick, so much so that when we got married I didn't know there would be future problems for the children. I had no idea that children born of a non-Jewish mother were not Jewish. How would I know? Aaron didn't tell me. Anyway, I was much more interested in his attitude toward Israel. He had come originally as a refugee in '48. He arrived, got a gun, and went straight into the '48 war. Very patriotic. But then he'd got *out,* and come to Oxford. This was in '58. And he wasn't sentimental the way other Israelis were. I kept meeting Israelis in London who said how much they loved London, but they were all bellyaching about getting home. They were a strange breed, a lot of ex-army officers and students, older students. I liked them, but they seemed a little brash. They were clannish—Israelis for Israelis. And they were constantly saying how awful the Jews were.

Aaron was going through his anti-Israel period. There were these endless *shlihim,* Israelis coming over to England on fund-raising and propaganda missions, and he would get up and attack them. Aaron would stand up at a public meeting and say—"And what about the *refugees?*"

Yet in a strange way, because he told me once that he never felt Hungarian, he remained a confirmed patriot. All the years we lived in Australia after we were married, he refused to give up his Israeli citizenship. People kept telling him how simple it was to get Australian citizenship, but he would not. Every year he insisted on going from Canberra or Melbourne to the consulate in Sydney to have his passport renewed.

Yet he never talked about living in Israel—I was the one who brought it up. In Dublin we had met some Israelis who were also all waiting for the time they could go home, and I began to think about Israel as a place that must be very nice to call "home." Because I didn't belong anywhere. I didn't belong in India, I loved England but I was not English, I loved Dublin but was certainly not Irish. I thought, "All these people, all talking about belonging—it's very nice." There was something very appealing about their need to go back.

I wanted to visit. That was in 1962 when we were on our way to Australia. But Aaron said no. It wasn't until

'67, after the children were born, that the serious home-sickness began. We were in Australia during the Six Day War, and that was when I realized. He was impossible to live with. He was already quite old, well too old to be in the front line and hold a gun. There was nothing he could have done, but he suffered. It was almost pathetic. He was beside himself. He was anxious. The anxiety was extraordinary—I just didn't understand what was happening to him. All day long he listened to the radio. He was depressed. He was just not there. It was after that that I knew we would come to live here.

We came in '73. Before we left Australia, friends said to me, "Olivia, you'll save yourself a lot of trouble if you simply write 'Jewish' when you get there." "Why should I?" I asked. "I'm not Jewish." I wouldn't sign a piece of paper saying that, but as I said, it was written on the card anyway without my noticing. But when Aaron went to register Michael and Rachel, he insisted: "Look, they're not. Leave it blank." They were left blank.

There were no pressures on me. You see in a funny way I have never been excluded, people would accept me because I was outrageously a stranger. Or they would think me Jewish. Or Greek. Or Spanish. My maternal grandfather was Spanish and he married a woman who was half Armenian and half Portuguese. So I am Spanish, Armenian, and Portuguese on one side and Flemish, French, and partly Cornish on the other side—that's where the British comes in. My relatives went to India as indigo planters. I can pose as whatever I like. When I dress in a sari and behave like an Indian, I can be Indian.

At Jewish weddings nobody would know that I wasn't if not a nice Jewish girl, at least a Jewish girl. Now when I came here I would sometimes make a point of saying "but *I'm* not Jewish" to get a reaction. All I would get was, well, maybe surprise. You know. "We *have* to be here, but you—why you?" Standard reactions like that, but really, no pressures.

After about two years I decided I would convert. Michael's bar mitzvah was coming close and I went to a rabbi to make a formal application. If I converted to Judaism, the children, as minors, would automatically convert with me. I had to make an umbrella application because of the children. Then the whole thing broke down. I couldn't go through with it. Look, for me the central theme of life here is belonging, and I didn't belong. If I could formally say I was a Jew it would, I thought, stabilize me and overcome this awful yearning I had to leave. It was a gesture to Aaron—"Yes, I am willing to try." That was what I said.

The rabbi said, "You will have to take instruction and I will send you the appropriate lady." But the appropriate lady was very religious. She wanted total belief from me. I felt I couldn't go through with this hypocrisy, especially in a country where 80 percent of the people are not religious. I went to her twice, then I told Aaron I couldn't do it anymore. At this point we met another rabbi. He was also Orthodox but had extremely liberal views. "Of course you don't need to go to somebody who will tell you when to have sexual intercourse," he said. "But you will still have to come before the court. I will brief you." He gave me and Michael some passages to learn. I could *not* memorize these passages of scripture. I don't think I am that stupid but I just could not memorize the one thing that I had to memorize, the *Sh'ma Yisroel.* That's the one prayer they require you to say: "Hear O Israel, the Lord is ours, the Lord is one." It is the prayer they say before dying or whenever—the ultimate commitment of faith. I was not able to do it. So I dropped it altogether.

Michael went ahead and the rabbi was marvelous. He agreed to convert Michael on his own without rabbinical approval. He simply did it to alleviate future problems. He performed the ritual, and on the eve of his bar mitzvah Michael was by Jewish law officially converted. This is not a hundred percent kosher.

So that is how one of the children is Jewish and one is not. I have now reached a point where on principle I definitely do not want to convert.

People don't make me feel bad about being non-Jewish. I talked about this with Martin Buber's granddaughter Judith when she stood for Parliament. Judith Agassi and her husband have this strange association—he is Jewish all the way but she is not. When they came to be married there was a commotion, and she said, "How dare somebody suggest that I, Judith Agassi, am not Jewish!" The rabbi married them all the same. So I decided, "Hell. If that's all I need to stay in the country. . . ."

If you gave me a paper to sign now saying I am Jewish, I think I'd sign it. I really don't have any problems with Israel any more. None of my difficulties have had to do with the country, except perhaps one.

It happened at Michael's school. He was insanely upset. I've never seen him like this. After he had been converted, some child at school yelled at him, *Imha notsria!* ("Your mother's a Christian!"). Thrown at you like this it's like saying *dago* or *yid.* Here we go again, I thought. I mean Michael wasn't actually called a bloody Jew in Australia, but *here*—where there should be the maximum tolerance—here in this country of all countries he has to be called names.

Why do I say "in this country of all countries"? Because these are the people who have suffered most. Because I have an expectation of Jewish people as special people, I do. I expect them to be different. Aaron keeps telling me that they're just like everybody else—but they are not just like everybody else. It's interesting. If someone else, an outsider, says to me, "They're different," or "They're not like other people," I get irritated. I won't have it. Yet *I* say it.

I see it all round me. I see it in the houses, in the family prayers, in the traditions. I see it in this obsession everyone has to talk about "the situation." At parties there is no small talk, absolutely none. The art of light conversation is nonexistent. I know I keep on about "commitment," but they are so *specifically* committed. I've heard people say, "I have to listen to the news. If I don't, I get ill." Aaron's the same way. He has to listen, on the hour. The children get mad at him. Maybe I am simply envious, because in the name of that commitment people are willing to do almost anything. They talk about nothing else. In Australia people didn't talk only about Australia.

Mind you I find myself doing the same thing. I also like the concern there is here for one human being as a human being. Is that normal? I see it in the markets, in the Carmel, and the Shuk, where I love going. The other day I was thinking that I feel sort of liberated there among the Orientals. Aaron claims I'm becoming quite native. I don't think so, I just like communicating with these people.

Israeli men are also marvelously good for the female ego. There's this constant Mediterranean repartee, a sort of constant sexual play between males and females. It is quite amazing. I remember, before I came, a religious boss of mine said, "Do you know of any other country where a minister in the government is more famous for his sexual exploits than for anything else?" He said it jokingly, but I'm not being flippant. I'm quite serious. There is the most extraordinary male-female play here. It's very nice.

But I kick against the involvement, because I don't have it. I still don't have it.

I've changed my mind about a lot of things lately. For instance, I used to find it terrible that children at school were already aware of death as a reality. I talked to some of these youngsters and it got me right in the guts that they just appeared to accept the fact that in a year or two they would go into the army and they and their peers would quite possibly be among those who would be mown down in a war. Now I think at least it will cushion them and not let them be too optimistic about what life is about. I was thinking about Michael. He's still young, only fourteen—but still.

Now it doesn't bother me so much, although you live

with it from day to day. I don't dwell on it because if I did I'd go stark-raving bonkers—as a friend of mine did. She came from Australia, a German girl who had suffered through the wars in Europe and then emigrated to Australia. She came here and she broke down because in every dark-skinned fellow she saw a threatening Arab. She got on a plane, left her husband and children, and went back to Germany, of all places.

I don't think I would leave in the event of a war now. Michael may leave. He still has some deep-seated resentments against the place, because of me, I suppose. One has so many fears and hesitations, but sooner or later you have to face some sort of reality. If I think about my difficulties here, the basic decision I need to make probably didn't concern converting at all, but staying. It never occurred to me in Australia to leave my husband but it did occur to me here. He'll be very angry with me for saying this, but my husband's commitment is to Israel and mine is not. My commitment is to my husband, though perhaps eventually one day it will be to Israel as well. I don't belong. I still say it. Perhaps the real fear is selfish—perhaps my biggest fear is the fact that my children will be committed to a place to which I am not. They will be Israeli and I will never be.

9

Yuval Aloni

What happens when you leave a railway station? The train comes, you get on and go away. It's the same for me. The place we left behind was a railway station.

I was dressed in a long striped robe and a blue-and-white striped silk jacket, with frogging and embroidery, and an embroidered silk hat, a tall hat. I looked nice. I also had earlocks. I brought nothing with me.

We went on camels to Ta'izz and in Ta'izz we rented two trucks. Many poor Jews in Ta'izz were waiting, so we took them with us on the trucks. The only thing we took for ourselves were two holy books, the Torah scrolls. The second floor of our house was a synagogue —part was synagogue and part was sleeping quarters for Jews coming and going from place to place. We left everything—a three-story house, a gigantic house. We didn't sell anything, we gave away everything we had. Who would have bought it? Everyone was leaving.

We came to the transit camp at Aden and waited. We waited for days, weeks—it's irrelevant. When you have been waiting throughout eternity, the time is irrelevant.

People carried small things that would go inside their pockets, but nothing of value. For God's sake, why should we take impure things? If we had brought impure things, we would have defiled the holy country. We needed money for expenses, that's all, to pay baksheesh to the sheikhs along the way so we could pass through their domains. But it was difficult for the women to part with their jewels.

When the plane was in the air, it started to shake and rock. We thought it was a punishment from God. Then the rabbi went up and said, "This is because you are bringing with you money and gold like it was in Egypt." So the people threw their gold and jewels out of the plane. Don't you see? They had never seen a plane before.

On the plane we prayed and read the Torah. We weren't coming to Israel to have a good time. We were climbing the stairs of Redemption. What do you think it was, a wedding? It wasn't an earthly thing at all. In the Bible it is said that the Messiah will come and His word is: "I will take you on eagles' wings and bring you to the holy land." And the fact is that planes came. We didn't come on ships, we came on wings of eagles, as it was written.

The plane was a Dakota. I know that now, but I didn't know it then. Was I frightened? You don't understand. Why should I be frightened? You might as well ask me if the plane had a pilot. What do you want? There was no hand of man, no pilot, no mechanic. The Lord sent me wings. God forbid. You don't understand yet! The Lord sent us on wings of eagles to fulfill a prophecy. Can't you recognize a miracle for a miracle?

I don't know how many Jews came here from Yemen. The country was totally closed and enclosed. There were no roads for cars and no need for them. A European came to Yemen in danger of his life. I had never heard of Russia or Stalin, Hitler, or the Holocaust. I knew there was a country called Italy but only because we were exporting coffee and skins and one day we received Italian liras. We had a wardrobe full of Italian liras that were worth nothing.

I lived in a village of only Jews, one day's walk from Ta'izz, the capital city. In Yemen there was no difference between grown-up and child. We read the same books, we grew together. If I had asked my father how it was in the holy land, he would have answered, "Read the Song of Songs." But I knew the answer the same as he did. It was clear to me from the age of three, clear like the sun. The land of Israel was the land of honey and milk.

Carmel and Canaan, Ashkelon, Gilboa—all the names, I knew all the places. We used to get up at midnight to say the special prayers, the *tikun hatzot,* which according to belief elevated you personally toward the divinity and the holy places. Some people even went there.

We children often dreamt that we had been in Jerusalem. There were many stories about the sages, the holy people who made a *kefitzat haderech*—a leap across space. Friday they were in Yemen and Saturday they were in Jerusalem. For a sage like Rabbi Shabasi it goes without saying, it was accepted that on Shabbat he was in Jerusalem and spent the Lord's Day there. I had these dreams, too. Of course I didn't make the leap because I was not a sage. Don't you have dreams like this?

My ambition was to be the Clever Pupil, the very best pupil. Anybody could reach this status, rich or poor, because religion was the way of life. For instance, where I lived nobody made a living just by being a rabbi—the rabbi was also a merchant. The same for the slaughterer. Nobody made a living from his religious activity. That's the reason the life and religion developed together.

On Shabbat we would touch nothing green—no grass, no leaves. At five in the morning we went to the synagogue. The grown-ups were singing songs and reading from the Torah. And we were the children. We were just singing a bit and sitting all day learning Torah. It was a delight. Torah is natural, like eating.

What would have happened if I hadn't studied? Impossible. There was no such thing as not to study. There was no Yemenite child—male child—who was not good at reading the Torah, at reading the translations from the Aramaic, at reading the commentaries of Rashi. That's the difference between us Yemenites and *all* the other groups of Jews in the world. With us, a child who reads Torah reads it by himself—for himself. Now why can't the other Jews do this? Why does the *hazzan,* who leads the prayers in synagogue, have to read it for them? Because it is difficult.

The Torah is written without vowels and punctuation stops. It is forbidden to mark the vowels or touch the text. So we had to know everything. My father knew the whole Torah. He knew the whole Mishna. He knew everything by heart. People say that we still read the Book like in the days of the First Temple.

When I say we studied only religion, it was the same for the Arabs—they learned about their religion and we learned about ours. But we were less than they were, and ironically that is how we became rich.

We had no rights to the earth, no fields of our own. But we were merchants. Before the planting season, the Arabs would come to my father for seeds, and he would finance their planting and then receive a share of the crop. He was getting richer while they stayed on the same level. Just because we were inferiors. As inferiors, we were not entitled to pay tax. But the Arab was a privileged citizen and he had to pay tax.

I never felt inferior. Look how it goes: everywhere I went I had to be lower than an Arab in height. A Jew on a donkey could not pass an Arab on foot. God forbid that you were higher than he! We were not allowed to own a horse or wear a turban or carry a weapon, because these were symbols of nobility. We were not allowed to have any of the things that belonged to people who were proud and free. But being Jewish, in my eyes, makes me a thousand times, an infinity of times, higher. I'm the chosen one.

A long time ago when the King of Persia freed the Jews in Babylon and Ezra called on Jews everywhere to come back and rebuild Jerusalem, the Jews of Yemen refused to return because they said that would be anticipating the coming of the Messiah. So Ezra cursed them to remain in Yemen without peace and in suffering. We were in exile.

I was born in exile and I was told when I was born that I am an exile. My father had been told that, too. And his father. So we were in exile all the generations, that was our lot. All the time we were only waiting for the day of redemption. Yet we couldn't hurry it.

To hurry the day—it would be like disputing a judgment of the Lord. It would be like questioning truth itself.

I was in school when the day came. Nobody walked into the village and said, "Hola! The state of Israel is declared." None of us sat down and took a count and said, "Will we go? Won't we?" It wasn't like that. It was in the air. The news was immediate, instantaneous. For us it was the Messiah.

It came with the speed of light—without radio, without newspapers, without anything. It's a prophecy, I told you. It wasn't only my village. It was the whole nation —the whole Jewish nation in Yemen.

In Ta'izz we put as many people as we could on the trucks we had rented, but when we had loaded as many as we could, there were still hundreds of people walking. People walked for days, weeks. There were no maps. The desert was not charted. Some were beaten and robbed, but nothing happened to us until we got to Aden and my embroidered jacket was stolen. I cried at first, until my father reminded me that where we were going everything was provided for.

When we arrived we were taken to a transit camp and we couldn't believe our senses. I had never seen such a thing before: a spade, a Jew with a spade in his hand. They were working in a citrus grove, digging holes. Have you seen those immense holes they have to pump water? In Yemen we had slaves doing these things, not citizens.

The camp was awful. It was near Natanya on the coast, and as soon as we arrived it snowed—the first time in history in this region. Especially in our honor! We didn't know what snow was. We had just come from a tropical land where the rains came in the summer and the winter was shiny. We were in tents and they all collapsed. People ran screaming. We had no idea what to do.

I saw snow, I saw simple people. I saw that the reality is very different from the dream. I never imagined, for instance, that Jews would use the holy tongue of Hebrew for talking, everybody talking! In Yemen, Hebrew was only for praying. For talking we spoke Arabic. I was in shock.

We were taken to a settlement in Galilee and my father had to clean the site of stones, break rocks with a hoe. He collapsed. Yet he would not complain against the land. He found that everything was so different from the scriptures, yet he felt it was forbidden to voice complaints against the land—he accepted everything, and my father and I were in terrible conflict. I swung from one extreme to the other. My state of shock lasted six months, then when I awoke, I cut off my earlocks and threw away my *kipah.* I lost my religion completely. Now I have come to a position of balance.

I live here with myself, without problems. Everything that was ours, all our culture, we brought along. The land was not ours, so it stayed there. Even if I have lost my religion I have lost nothing of my country. Can you understand? My soul can never leave this place. I would never think of emigrating, never. To emigrate? You mean go *down*? What a question. You see, I care. I care very much that my people should be continued. I was a second-class citizen. It is a thing you cannot forget. Here the land is ours and it does not matter if it is good—it is like a man and his son. If the son is not so good, so what. Will he kill him? Certainly if I had stayed in Yemen I would now be a rich rabbi and not have to go to war. Wars, what difference does that make? I am going to breakfast or I am going to war, for me it is just the same. In '67 I was in the Six Day War and in '73 in the Yom Kippur War, I fought in tanks. In '56 they said I was too young to go into a fighting unit, so I went to jail until they let me.

My sons will go to war like I did. Of course, I expect it. The fact that I don't wear a *kipah* or pray any more doesn't mean that certain things haven't broken into me, like the Prophets, the Justice, the Truth—these are in my blood, not just in my head. I expect much more from this people than any other. In Yemen, for example, I will pay bribes like anyone else, because the Arab is lord of the universe and corruption is accepted. But here, in Israel, if I see anything that has even a whiff of corruption, I will shout my lungs out, I will go out of my mind. Anywhere else if someone avoids the draft, so what. Here, if someone even dreams of that, it becomes for me horribly "anti-moral." That is why in '56 the army put me in jail. I wanted to be a tankist, but the army decided I had the profile to be a youth leader. I thought that was shameful. I had to refuse for a whole month, until I was accepted into the armored corps.

You may think that my inner life has changed, but you are wrong if you think it has changed severely. This morning I went to my father's house and I saw him reading the Texts. I read with him and he was happy to hear that I read correctly, accurately, beautifully. He enjoyed it very much. I read the *Parasha,* the *Aftarah.* Everyone sat down and was happy. Shalom! Did I drive? Yes, and driving is forbidden on the Sabbath. I always drive to my father's house on Shabbat, but I come in the back way and no one sees me, or rather they pretend they don't. But inside my father's house I break no rules. Everything is ordained and clear, down to the smallest detail. There is no problem that you meet that does not have its own clear rules. My father taught me to read, and this morning, as I was reading after him, everybody was listening to the pitch of our voices because it has a particular meaning. When my father made a mistake I *had* to correct him, but very gently. It is an obligation to correct him, but very modestly, and he in turn must acknowledge his mistake. In this way we are different from the other Orientals where everything that the father says is consecrated.

In the beginning we were only a few Yemenite families, now there are sixty families on the moshav—from Greece, from Turkey, from Poland, from Persia, from Russia, from India, from Canada, from Rumania, from Iraq, from Algeria, from Morocco, from everywhere. It is cooperative. Everyone sweats in his private field, yet all decisions are taken democratically.

I am very involved in the politics of the moshav movement and I fight for it because I care about it. In another society what would I care about? It does not matter that on the moshav as a farmer I am losing money. That is my choice. That is how I believe it must be for reasons of principle. Here I have an expectation, I can influence the way of life. So we can build a kibbutz, a moshav, a moshav shitufi, a city—all modes of settlement, whatever we want. We are a small country with very few people and we have more modes of settlement than any place in the world.

Next year I am starting an open university, a branch of the State University of New York, especially for moshavniks. I am the first student. You know what it means? It is not simple. You come from a feudal society, like it was in Europe in the twelfth century. You go through a lot, something like two hundred and eighty generations in a lifetime—it's not simple! I feel like somebody who has lived for seven hundred years.

10

David Karon

They knew more than we did. They were a huge book to study.

You could see a village of eight hundred inhabitants, with no school, and no doctor; you could see them being exploited by a few feudals and accepting their fate without protest. For me it was something new, something fascinating. It was absolutely different from anything I had known. I could not see a single point of sameness with this society. Wait. I could hear an echo of history. Sometimes, instead of an ox, the farmer would put his wife in the collar to plow with the donkey. And I remembered that the Talmud says you should not plow with a donkey and an ox, because they are not equal forces and the donkey will exploit the ox. Watching the Arabs in the fields, these lessons from school in Poland came alive to me. But only as an echo of history.

They knew about rain, about the dew also. They knew that when the rains stop in April, the dew continues to bring water to the night-growing plants. When we came we had no drop of irrigation, no cup of shade. They gave us the correct seeds to plant.

In one of these villages nobody owned any land—if you were born there, your share was born with you; if you died, it died with you. The village was divided up for cropping, so no man went hungry. It was a system of primitive communism going back to biblical times. But there was the vendetta, eh, where you could kill a man, provided you paid for the blood. I remember a man saying, "Thanks be to God, this year I have a good crop. Now I can kill my enemy because I have the wheat to pay the price."

There were three villages. All our land was bought from these three Arab villages surrounding our settlement, some thousands of people. Where are they now?

They have run away. Their mud houses have dissolved with the rain and most of it turned back into fields. They have all run away except Abu, the old man of Telesafi.

When we came, we were the farthest Jewish settlement in the south. I was the watchman. My job was to guard the fields because the Bedouin would raid us—the old battle between the nomad and the settlers. This was the border. We were townspeople, but we could defend ourselves. Sure, we were a kibbutz. Our trouble was we were starving. We had no income—all we had was a tractor.

So I went plowing for Abu and the other Arab landowners. This was the first income for the kibbutz. The Arabs made it a point of honor to feed us well. We were working for them, enjoying fried chicken while the kibbutz itself was starving. The kibbutz had failed once, in 1936. We came in 1939. If it had not been for Abu we might also have failed, but we made plenty of money plowing for the Arabs. For years it was the biggest income for the kibbutz.

Abu was a big landowner, a sheikh and an important personality. He had two wives and many sons. We spent many days together on horseback, and it is from him that I learned Arabic. There was a time in '42 when the Germans were pushing toward Cairo—and if Cairo fell, Palestine would be next—when every morning Abu would appear and gaze into the south. One morning when I was guarding the fields he said, "Don't worry, David. When the Germans come, we will hide you." Only me, and not the others on the kibbutz. It was a bitter thing to hear.

All this time we had Arab friends coming and going from the kibbutz. We had one Arab neighbor who in '47 used to come every day with his pickup to bring us ammunition he had bought from the British. Sometimes he came twice a day. He knew the risk, but he trusted us.

If the Arab governments had accepted a Palestinian state when it was offered to them in 1947, we would not now have a refugee problem.

The trouble started at the crossroads, at a big village called Mesmiya, which was the border between the two states under the 1947 partition plan. Egyptians from Gaza began to infiltrate Mesmiya and all the villages around us. Abu was not living in a village but in a big house on the land. We went to him. "Abu, listen. There is going to be a battle. We're going to take you and your family to a safe place, all of you. After the battle you can come back again. What do you say?"

The old man never hesitated. "Take everything," he

said. "Take everything I have and keep it for me." He gave all his belongings to the kibbutz, including three tractors that he had. Then all of a sudden he looked round and his family was not there. On a certain morning the whole village of Mesmiya emptied itself, scared out by the Egyptian propaganda: "Whoever stays is a Jewish slave and will be killed with the Jews. Go away and you can return with the victorious Egyptian army!" It was harvest time. They left the wheat and the barley, this mass of people from Mesmiya, and they carried with them the inhabitants of the smaller villages who were hesitating, including Abu's whole family, his three brothers and their wives, their sons, his sons, his wives —everything. Abu remained the sole human being there.

Then Abu went away, and because I had no money to give him, no cash, I gave him the only thing I had that he could sell for good money, my pistol. I never thought I would see him again.

After the first round of fighting was over I was called back from the Negev to Jaffa, which was an occupied city.

One day, walking in the streets in Jaffa, I heard my name. It was the old man. My God, we both wept. He came to my office and we talked. I had taken over the former office of the Lebanese consul and was working for military intelligence, running agents over the border. Abu said his family had fled to Jordan. I promised him that when I had a chance I would bring one of the children to him. And I did.

You know what it is for a mother to send a child—a

boy, a favored son—through the border at night just because a Jew called David has said, "Come"? The mother was in Jordan. And I did not go myself. An officer of mine met the boy, smuggled him through, and brought him to my house. Younes was thirteen, but absolutely quiet and confident. He slept with me, and the next morning I took him to his father.

But the family was scattered, in Jericho, in Bethlehem, some in Hebron. At first, after they ran away from Telesafi, they had lived in caves. But Abu remained in Jaffa, alone. Only once in those twenty years from 1948 to 1967 was he able to arrange a meeting with his sons, at the Mandelbaum Gate, which was dividing Jerusalem. But he told me he was so overcome with emotion that he came away without talking to them.

Eventually Abu returned to Telesafi, and the kibbutz received him like a brother. But because we had become a state and inherited a bureaucracy from the British, Abu had no title to his land. The old man demanded his land and his house, but he had nothing to show to prove his ownership. So I dictated a list of his holdings for the authorities—he had here and in the Negev many hundreds of acres. And because of this document Abu got his land back, then his house. He got his tractors back, too. No, I am wrong—the army had commandeered the tractors. For the tractors he was paid compensation.

Shortly afterward his family came—his wives, his sons, his daughters, and all the grandchildren. And here they remain.

When Abu died—he was killed in a car accident—our oldest boy, Yehuda, was away in the army, but he took leave so he could come to the funeral. As a little boy

Yehuda would climb onto Abu's knee and call him *grandpa.* For me it was a matter of simple human relations, but for Yehuda it was more than that, because neither my wife nor I have parents in Israel.

During the '73 war, when one of the children of the kibbutz was killed, the family of Abu's son Younes came to the funeral. It was a military funeral with full honors, yet the Arab family felt not only obliged but confident to come, although the boy was killed in a war against the Arabs. A war with the Arabs has nothing to do with the people here, nothing to do with local relations.

Listen. If one of my neighbors joins the PLO, it does not mean the Arab citizens of Israel are enemies of mine. If Israel is at war with Egypt, it does not mean this Arab neighbor is my enemy. That is a wrong way to think— "those Arabs." Only ignorant people think like this. This is no way to understand one another even if we are at war with an Arab state. But, see, I must make this clear to you.

In 1956, after the Suez campaign, we held a couple of hundred Egyptian officers as prisoners. We had two camps, one for the low-ranking officers and another for the high ones from lieutenant colonel up. I was responsible for interrogating the younger officers. It was our first meeting since Nasser's revolution in 1952, and there was a feeling that maybe Egyptian society was changing under the Nasser regime. The Egyptians are friendly by nature, they like to laugh and joke. The most anti-Nasser jokes I have ever heard, I learned from these Egyptian prisoners.

I was called to the other camp where there was a senior officer, a full colonel, who had refused to talk to anyone. I could see he was a very proud man but gravely depressed and, you know, struggling inside. "What is eating you?" I said.

"Some personal problems. None of your business." Finally he told me that he was distraught over what had happened to his daughter—the little girl had been struck dumb from shock when our soldiers had taken him from their home in Gaza. He was the attorney general of the Egyptian forces in Gaza. So I went there and found his wife and little girl living in a camp we had made for the families. You know that all khaki looks the same, children can't tell the difference. The little girl came bouncing up on my knee, chattering away. She was in good shape. I brought back a letter for the colonel from his wife and, well, he was a happy man.

After our initial interrogations were over, we wanted to do something with these prisoners. If you want, you may call it indoctrination. These Egyptians were absolutely ignorant about Israel. To them Jewish people were people with horns, not human beings. We decided to take the prisoners for a tour throughout the country so they could meet and talk to Jews. "Would you like to see your wife and daughter?" I asked the colonel.

"What do you mean?"

"I'm inviting you out. I will take you to my home, and I will bring your family along so we can spend the day together." We were living in a shack then, a two-room apartment. I brought the colonel home one evening and early the next morning I left to fetch his wife and daughter. When we arrived back at the kibbutz, I left the family alone together to say whatever they had to tell one another.

Later I showed the colonel around the kibbutz. In the cattle shed I introduced him to a man equal to him in rank who was milking cows. He refused to believe it. He couldn't understand it at all, an Israeli colonel milking cows! In the Egyptian army the gap between officers and soldiers is so big it leads to disaster. The officers care so little for their men that if they are pressed they just abandon them.

"Do the people know I am an Egyptian officer?"

"Certainly," I said. He was in full uniform, with his braid and cap. He had to wear the cap because of his dignity and rank.

"You know what I have noticed," he said. "I have noticed maybe curiosity on their faces, curiosity and wonder, but I have noticed no hate."

I took him all through the kibbutz without having warned anyone in advance. To the schoolrooms, the ceramics factory, the chickens, all over.

In the afternoon, when our children came home, they played with his little girl. We explained to them that these people were our guests and that the little girl was living in a camp. Yehuda was nine, Ezra six, about the same age as the girl. They played together on the floor with puzzles. Ezra asked, "Can we give her some things since she has no toys?"

"Whatever you want."

So they gave her some gifts. Then she said, "Papa, when will the two boys come to see us in Cairo?" When she said this, we—the grown-ups—just lowered our heads.

When I was growing up, there was never any doubt that I would come to Palestine. I never felt like an intruder here, because the background I brought with me protected me. In Poland I was always an unwanted citizen. The population was basically Russian. We lived in the Russian part, not the ghetto. Many times we were afraid to go to school because the native boys would attack us and beat us very badly. I learned to fight back early, but the kids from the ghetto thought I was strange, because their nature was to run away. I never felt that I should give up and go back to live there as a refugee.

I remember when I was young, playing with the native boys—the natives were Russians, White Russians. I was just like them, only black-haired and they were blond. One boy said, "Tell me, what is a Jew?"

"Jew is a nation, a nationality," I told him.

"Do you have land?"

"Not that I know of."

"Do you grow bread?"

"No."

"What kind of a nation is that then?"

I was nine, maybe ten.

The Yiddish Jews from the ghetto would tease me. They'd say, "What are you going to grow in Palestine, horseradish? Raisins and horseradish—this will be your big export, eh?"

All the youth movements like mine had the same basic idea—to reconstruct a nation of Jews producing like normal people and not living only as middlemen. There were fifty-five of us in the youth movement, but only six got to Palestine. All the rest went down the drain with Hitler.

I was sixteen when I arrived in 1930. Toni came after me, in 1939, from Cologne. She was smuggled ashore at night from a ship. There was some legal trouble when we decided to marry, because I had forgotton that I already had a wife. In 1935, after I had been in Palestine five years and could get a British passport, I immediately went back to Poland and married a girl from the same youth movement. Because of the immigration quota, she couldn't get a visa on her own, but she could come to Palestine as the "wife" of a passport holder. Unfortunately you couldn't marry just any pretty girl you liked in the movement, you had to take the one on top of the list. I was lucky. My girl—the one I "married"—was a good girl. She lives here on the kibbutz. Her husband— her present husband—came a bit later, with another "wife." Of course the British knew. They are not so stupid. But what could they do?

I didn't hate the British, not even when they came to this kibbutz searching for arms and making arrests. Who do you hate? People you don't know. People you don't meet.

Religious people won't agree with a word I say—I don't pray, I don't keep kosher, I don't do a single thing I should do. I am a bad Jew. Ezra, my son, says I have inherited the prophets' belief in justice. Okay, I believe in justice. You can put it in the frame of religion if you want. You know about the Gentile who said to the rabbi, "Teach me how to be a Jew while I am standing on one foot." The rabbi said, "This is the whole story: *Love your fellow man as yourself. All the rest is commentary.*" If you want to believe this is the whole story, I am certainly a Jew. But I don't succeed very well—I bear grudges. There are Jews on this kibbutz I haven't spoken to for years. In my relations with people, I am closer to our Arab neighbors at Telesafi than to some people here.

I don't feel bitter toward the Jordanians because of what they did in Jerusalem. During their occupation of the city, they completely destroyed the Jewish quarter, including the ancient synagogues. On the Mount of Olives they took up gravestones to make paths and even put headstones down in the mud in the lavatories so that people wouldn't dirty their feet. I don't find this so terrible, because these are the headstones of dead people. They are dead stones. It is not even a question of forgiveness.

You can take revenge on people, you can't take revenge on governments. I mean you can forgive or not forgive, but there is no point in not forgiving a government, because it is a temporary thing. Especially an Arab government.

11

Oula el-Aziz

In all my years at high school, I never made a Jewish friend. We didn't sit together; there were no social gatherings. In four years, we didn't have a single outing together. It was a shock, because for as long as I could remember, I had been fighting to go to this school in Haifa where Arabs and Jews could mix.

All my life I had wanted to study. I loved studying. At home, back in the village, we used to gather every morning at a quarter to eight in the rented rooms that served for a school. As soon as the headmaster came, he would tell us a story and then ask questions. Because I loved studying, I usually knew the answers, and since I was such a very small girl, the whole school would cheer me on. When I went away to high school, I was the only girl in the class. At that time it was difficult to be admitted at the first attempt. I was told that when the news reached my village, people gave out sweets and oranges. And when my father heard, he sent more sweets. The whole school celebrated. Even years later, when I walked through the village, I'd see the children pointing and whispering, "That's the one that passed matriculation. That's the one that passed matriculation."

Living in a family with ten children, in two rooms, having to share everything, there was no little corner I could call my own. There was no electricity, no running water. There was no desk, but I did have a notebook. I used to write on the floor. At night I used an oil lamp, which smoked and hurt my eyes. The smell of it gave me headaches.

I had always been encouraged—first by my father and then by the headmaster. But when I wanted to go to university, the headmaster was annoyed. He began to visit my father at night, saying, "Why send her to university? What's the point? She's only a girl." In Bir Zaytun it just wasn't customary for a girl to live outside the village or go to university. It wasn't done. There were several other girls who might have gone on to high school with me but they didn't. Instead they got married and stayed in Bir Zaytun. All my brothers except one have stayed in the village.

My father was an only son, an orphan. He had to fend for himself because he inherited nothing and nobody gave him anything. When he was small he wouldn't study and ran away from school. He became a shopkeeper but could hardly manage his accounts. But we benefitted from his lack of learning. He gave us, especially me, the chance he never had. Was he unusual? For a Moslem Arab, this was very unusual.

But when I wanted to go away, to leave the village and study at the university in Haifa, I had to fight with my father as well as the headmaster. I had to fight for the right to sleep outside the village. University classes don't end before evening, and if I missed the evening bus I had to wait hours for another, which meant I didn't get home until midnight. My father would wait for me in the street, in winter. This went on for two months. Then my father got very cold and finally gave in. Actually it was my mother who finally convinced him. In Haifa I took a room with an Arab family. My mother had to come and check that there were no sons in the house and to see what kind of family it was. There was another girl rooming in the house who was also at the university. Whenever we met, she greeted me in Hebrew. Also, classes were given in Hebrew. One day a lecturer introduced us formally to each other, and I discovered that she was also an Arab. She was from a village in upper Galilee, farther north than mine. We were both surprised. Until then neither of us had thought there *could* be another Arab girl at Haifa University.

All this time the headmaster was working against me. Next to the *mukhtar* he is the most powerful man in the village. He kept telling my father, "Don't send her to university. Send her to teachers college." If I had gone to teachers college as he wanted, he would have had a ready-made teacher in two years. He was short of teachers. Also, I was his favorite pupil. While I was in elementary school he paid us the compliment of teaching history himself. I tried to please him. He had studied in Jerusalem during the British mandate and had a good command of the English language, so he used to translate English books into Arabic. You see, we had no textbooks. There was a syllabus laid down by the Ministry of Education, but there were no books to learn from. Only the teacher had a book, which was usually in Hebrew or English, and this he would translate word for word to the class. After school the headmaster would take his notes and go home, and I had the great honor of staying at school each night and dictating his lecture to the rest of the class. The trouble was that the head-master prepared only one chapter at a time. In this way I learned about World War I and then about World War II. When we had finished the Second World War, I thought I would surprise him. I cleaned the blackboard and wrote a beautiful big headline for the next day's lesson: WORLD WAR III. That's the kind of schooling we had.

Even today in some villages there are still no Arabic textbooks. My old headmaster is still there and I don't think he would approve of any changes. Perhaps another reason that he tried to stop my going to university was that he feared I might get my degree before he did. And so I did.

The first Jews I remember meeting were from a kibbutz. Once a year these kibbutz people would come to my village, and we always took in someone. Not everybody wanted to put up Jews—some people were afraid—but there was a spot in the village where the *mukhtar* would bring them, and my father was always first in line to take someone in. The Jews came to meet the Arabs. It was a bit one-sided though, because they never invited us back. Yet we liked each other, and I got a very positive impression of Jews and so I thought all Jews were good because these people were kind enough to visit us. They couldn't speak Arabic and we couldn't speak much Hebrew, but they kept in touch and wrote us letters afterward in very simple Hebrew.

When I went to high school in Haifa I met a totally

different kind of Jew. It was the only school in our area where Jews and Arabs studied together, and I thought, "At last I will have a chance to meet more Jews." As I said, it was a shock. These Jews ignored me. Not only did we not study together, but even on the playground we were separated. My younger brother, who started after me, found the same thing and dropped out altogether. He couldn't take it.

To go to Haifa I had to leave home at five o'clock in the morning. I would arrive at half-past five although school didn't begin until eight. Sometimes I would get there before the janitor, yet I didn't mind. I just went in and caught up on my homework. I was happy because I had electricity and a desk. The school was locked, but that didn't matter. I was on good terms with the janitor. When school ended, I had to run hard all the way to try to catch the bus. But I usually missed it anyway and had to wait four hours for the next one. At the bus station, people sat and talked to me. They took me for a Yemenite—I mean a Yemenite Jew—because although I am dark I'm not that dark. Naturally they took me for a Jew. What nice Arab girl would sit alone in a public place and talk to strangers? One man who had seen me talking to the *mukhtar,* the head of the village who was wearing a kaffiyeh, sat down next to me and said, "What's the matter with you? Why do you talk to a man like this?" I said, "I'm that kind, too. I'm also an Arab." He obviously thought Arabs were people with tails.

Until I was fifteen I wasn't aware I was growing up in a Jewish land at all. Everything around me was Arab. There were other Arab girls just as smart as I was, but they couldn't continue with their education. Everyone has such big families, and the families always calculated: "Since we can't afford to send more than one or two to study, it had better be a boy." Our society revolves around the man, because the son is the one who is going to inherit the land and continue the line, so the son is considered the better investment. A girl is no good because she leaves home. A son stays. It's a great honor to have a son, and you always call a father after his first son. If the son's name is Ibraham, you call the man Abu Ibraham, Ibraham's father. But if you have only daughters, it's something shameful. Even if I were the eldest child, my father would *never* be called Abu Oula, after me.

One man in the village had only daughters, thirteen daughters. But he was optimistic. He kept on trying for the desired son. Only the son never arrived. He was known as *Abu-l Banat,* the father of daughters—not a very complimentary title. In fact, in the Arabic department of Hebrew University where I am now, all the professors in my department are Jewish and nearly all of them have only daughters. So the whole department is known as the "Faculty of Daughters." Last year when I became pregnant again, one of the teachers in the department who has only daughters said to me, "Change departments quickly, Oula, or you'll have another daughter." But I didn't change and now I have another daughter. So there you are.

I don't know when it was that I realized I was worth less than a boy. Growing up in Bir Zaytun I saw it all around me, but I didn't notice it. I saw the other girls doing what was expected of them, getting engaged at fifteen and married by twenty. If you are not married by twenty, a man won't have you. They didn't protest—they knew it was a lost battle to begin with. In a girl stubbornness isn't a virtue. Obedience is a virtue.

Did I have a nickname? Not that I can remember.

Well, actually, I was called after the old woman Chouri, the stubbornnest woman in the village.

But you couldn't talk back. If the teacher screams at you, you keep quiet. You couldn't have an idea that was different from his. It's like this in the home, too—whatever the parents say is right.

The greatest sin of all is to damage the family honor. This is why it is good to come from a big family with many sons, because it means better protection for the family honor. There was a case two weeks ago. An Arab girl was betrothed to a certain boy, but his family broke it off because the marriage contract wasn't satisfactory. However, the girl continued to receive love letters from the boy. So her brothers went to the boy's house and killed his father—simply because the family honor was at stake. Cases like this are in the newspapers all the time.

So what was expected of me as a daughter? To be pretty, to be a good cook, to run the house, and serve my husband. And bear sons.

Have I come a long way since I used to write on the floor? From a village school to university in Haifa to Hebrew University. When I came to Jerusalem I enrolled in a course taught by a very famous professor I wanted to study with, a Polish Jew. He is very scornful, and sometimes tells people who come from Haifa to "go away and play marbles"—that's his attitude toward people like me who come from provincial places. The first day I walked into his class he said, "Who are you?" "I'm first year," I said. "Then what are you doing in my class? Get out." Obediently, I picked up my books and left. He thought I was a first-year undergraduate. But one of the other students who knew me called out, "Professor, she's first-year *M.A.*!" So he ran into the corridor and fetched me back.

He's the sort of man I hoped to study with all along, he's like a father. Not only to me, to everyone. "If you're after an M.A.," he said to me, "you'd better take a subject that can be done in a couple of years, because if you stay with me it can take half a lifetime." But I stayed with him and I'm glad. I also finished my M.A., and I'm only twenty-eight or twenty-nine—we're not quite sure.

This year I ran for the Knesset. I don't know if I am the first Arab woman in Israel to do these things, but I suppose I must be. I don't like to talk about myself this way. I just know that I am considered among the first generation of educated Arab women. But you can't take too big a leap or you'll fall down. I wouldn't even say that I have succeeded, because what I really wanted to do was social work but I was too young to enroll in the proper course of study, so I took classical Arabic instead.

My husband comes from a village not far from mine. We went to university together in Haifa. We're both Moslems although neither of us is religious. We don't observe the rituals like praying and fasting, but on the other hand we don't break any religious laws either. I believe in the Koran. I believe there is one God and that Mohammed is his prophet. But Mohammed wasn't just a prophet, he was also a social reformer and innovator. He was the first to reform the status of women in the Arab world. Before Islam, newborn girls were buried alive. Mohammed forbade this in the Koran. He was the first nationalist.

In Islam there is a whole literature of stories and sayings about those who were "the first" to do anything. Is it a virtue to be first? Yes. But I don't like to talk about myself in this way. You see, it is only a virtue if it does not offend Islam.

All I know is that once I started studying I knew I would go on. I've loved it and I've wanted it and I've *done* it, so in an academic sense I have succeeded. And I'm very lucky to be in Jerusalem. It is important for me to live in East Jerusalem, in an Arab neighborhood. But still, you can be isolated from your own kind.

What about my children, will they go to an Arab school? That's just it. I don't know. Aisha is now in a Jewish kindergarten. I have doubts about sending her to an Arab school because I don't think Arab schools have changed that much. So I'm in conflict. I want a good school for my daughters, on the other hand I want them to have Arab culture with Arabic their mother tongue— even though, as you see, I am talking to you now in Hebrew. I find it very difficult talking to you like this anyway, but in some ways I can express myself better in Hebrew. One thing I do know: I want my daughters to have it easier than I did.

What does it *mean* to be an Israeli Arab? It means that out of Israel I am a stranger. It means that I belong here —my family has been here for generations. It means that even though you're only five miles from your village, you can be a refugee. Being an Israeli Arab is a problem we all have to face, even Aisha.

At first Aisha attended the Hebrew University kindergarten on the campus where we were living. She spoke a mixture of Arabic and Hebrew. But she already knows to whom she's expected to speak Arabic and to whom Hebrew. She learned this when she was four. Now she is going to a higher kindergarten in French Hill, a Jewish suburb. When I registered her, the teacher looked at the birth certificate and saw the name, Aisha Abud, and said to me, "Are you Arab?" I said yes. "Moslem?" "Yes." "What are *you* doing here?" I told her she shouldn't have asked me that question.

This is why I became interested in politics. I belong to a party that stands for coexistence between Jews and Arabs.

We are much more aware of the Jewish people than they are of us. Of course. We start school and learn their language and about their national poets and their culture, but most Jews don't study Arabic at all. And if they do, they only study literary or newspaper Arabic, which isn't how to talk. Without the language how far can they get?

I lived here on the campus for three years in young couples' dorms where there were children. We were one Arab family—me and my husband and our first child— living among twenty-two Jewish families. Next to us was a young couple: Carmel was studying philosophy and her husband was a geologist. My husband and I are both dark, and Carmel assumed that we were Yemenite Jews. After Aisha was born, my mother came to help me. When Carmel saw my mother she realized by the way she was dressed that we were Arabs. She went inside and locked the doors and windows, in case we might come after her. She was quite petrified. She did this for three months, until we all moved out of the dormitory and into asbestos huts on the road to Ramallah. Now we had open space and grass. In order to go to classes we had to baby-sit for each other. Carmel also had a full-time job and at one point she couldn't find a nurse for the baby, so since I wasn't working I offered to keep her baby for a week. When I wouldn't accept payment, she was surprised. That's when she started changing her attitude.

And let me tell you, children repeat the generalizations of their parents. I believe there are good Jews and bad Jews, but Jewish children tend to grow up thinking that all Arabs are bad. At kindergarten, for example, Aisha represents the good Arab. Last month when they celebrated Independence Day the children were shouting things like "kill the Arabs." The teacher pulled them aside and pointed to Aisha as an example of a good Arab. Since then she has made more and more friends in kindergarten.

Coming back at night, Carmel was afraid to get off the bus on the Ramallah road in case she met an Arab. "I'm afraid of an Arab," she'd say, "because he's a stranger." Me, I'm afraid of strangers because they are strangers, but for her it is fear of strangers *because they are Arabs.* So I just remind her of the time she used to lock her door against me and how we've since become friends. We go to Carmel's place a lot, or they will come to us—we've been friends now for five years. We talk and talk. What about? Usually about the Jewish-Arab conflict.

How can one live five miles from home and be a refugee? It isn't *being* a refugee, it's what you are *made to feel*. The trouble is being a minority within your own kind. What's a refugee? A refugee is what they call you. Palestinian Arabs living in Egypt or Syria have it pointed out to them all the time. You feel you're a refugee because people point it out to you. *Refugee*, it's like a swear word.

Arabs who didn't return after the War for Independence are not accepted back into Israel. This is why if we —my family I mean—had stayed in Lebanon, it would have been awful.

There we would have been refugees. For all I know I was born a refugee in Lebanon, because although my papers say I was born in 1948, my mother says it was 1947. But she isn't sure. At that time they didn't register each baby individually. To save trouble, people waited till they had a few and registered them together. This is what my mother did. In the war, when many Arabs fled to Lebanon, our family ran away but then came back. The only one who stayed in the village was my grandmother.

In some villages they ran because they were chased out, in others they simply ran. My husband's entire village was one family, about seven hundred people, and they all left. Some of them are now government ministers in Jordan and Syria. This is why you can't expect

Israeli Arabs to join the army and fight for Israel, against other Arabs, against our own kind.

So should this be one country or two? My feeling is one country for two peoples, Arabs and Jews. If an American Jew is willing to leave his country and come here for some historical reason, if he feels this to be his home, fine. But I—I who was born here and have my roots here—I am not accepted.

During the Six Day War, near the university campus, two or three Arabs were killed. Now at every festival, our neighbors bring a wreath and lay it beside the pit where they are buried. Once, after one of these festivals, a new Jewish neighbor, an extremist, knocked at my door. "What are they doing?" he said. I explained. He began to scream. "They shouldn't do that. They are our enemies!" he said, shouting at me as if I were to blame and claiming that Mayor Kollek had forbidden this kind of thing. "You go to Teddy Kollek and you tell him that," I said. This is the Israeli Arab as seen by the Jew.

Two months later there was another Arab festival. Outside my house I saw two Jerusalem Arab women carrying flowers and a ribbon with an inscription. The inscription was a verse from the Koran. I went closer to read the words. "Do not consider those who died for the sake of God as dead but as living still. And may they enjoy Heaven." "What's this?" I said. "It's to spite you," one of them said, thinking I was Jewish. "These are martyrs who died fighting against you. They're martyrs, whether *you* like it or not." This is the Israeli Arab as seen by another Arab.

The Israeli Jews don't accept us and the Jerusalem Arabs don't accept us. We're caught between the two.

Since '67 many Israeli Arabs have come to East Jerusalem and have managed to convince Jerusalem Arabs that they are not traitors but are in fact better Arabs because they stayed and didn't run away. Running away is shameful. Was what my family did in running away to Lebanon shameful? But they came back.

It was my mother who insisted not only that we had no business to be in Lebanon but that we must come back. My father was frightened so she took four of us and came back to the village, to Bir Zaytun, on her own. A few months later she walked all the way back to Beirut on foot, day and night, and brought him and the other children home. So we owe it to her that we all came back.

My mother is still in the village. I ring her every day from Jerusalem, or she will ring me. I have always wanted to be in Jerusalem, and where we live at the moment, in East Jerusalem, is very fine, very beautiful— a fine Arab suburb. Still it's lonely, I'm even lonely in this neighborhood. We keep very much to ourselves. I've lost touch with school friends; nearly all my friends now are Jewish.

We've talked of moving, perhaps to French Hill or Ramat Eshkol. They're both Jewish suburbs. If we moved, I don't think I would want it to be to another Arab neighborhood. It's difficult to live without friends.

12

Robert Mimouni

I find that for some people the world will do everything, and for others, less. Last year, my son Jean-Jacques rescued a dog that had had its paw crushed. He made a splint, and the animal recovered. Then one day, as he came to feed it, the dog sprang past him into the street and was killed by a passing car. Jean-Jacques buried it on the street by a tree. After Entebbe, I told this to our mayor. "This street isn't named," I said. "Why not call it after my son?"

"What a good idea," the mayor said. "Of course, the council will have to think it over." That was a year ago. They are still thinking it over. Today my son, my only son, would have been twenty.

He was the sixth child. My wife already had five children, all girls. We both prayed for a son. In Tunisia, where I come from, it is a dishonor not to have a son. I was on duty at headquarters when the doctor at the hospital rang. It was one o'clock in the morning.

My colleagues had been teasing me for weeks. "A girl, a girl," they said. "It will only be another girl."

"No, this time it will be a boy."

"You'll see, another girl—six in a row."

But I was sure it would be a boy.

"All right, if it's a boy," they said, "you must take off your uniform and parade down the main boulevard in your underwear." If they had asked me to jump out of a fifth-floor window, I would have said yes.

When the doctor rang and said it was a boy, I asked the deskman to telephone my colleagues and get them out of bed. Then I took off my tunic, my pullover, shirt, trousers—the nights are cold in Tunis in December—and ran outside. At the last moment I was ashamed to be seen walking undressed down the Centrale Avenue, so I took one of the station bicycles. I was a senior policeman. Everyone in Tunis knew me. I got on the cycle and pedalled the length of the Centrale Avenue in my under-pants. Even at that hour there were people. They all stared.

Then I thought, "What if he's putting me on?" The doctor who had called was the one who had delivered my five daughters, and it suddenly hit me he might be joking. I rode back to headquarters, got in my car, and rushed to the hospital. "He's putting me on," I said to Lola, my wife.

"But Robert," she said. "It really *is* a boy."

I wouldn't believe it until I had proof with my own eyes. I made them take off all the covers and when I saw that it really was a boy, I grabbed the doctor and kissed him on the mouth.

I knew it would be a boy because in our family it was always "five plus one," the Mimouni fate. My father had five boys and then a girl. My older brother had five boys and then a girl. Another brother the same. So after five daughters, I knew the next would be a boy. We called him Jean-Jacques.

He was fifteen when we came to Israel. The decision to come here was made by the children after we had left Tunisia and moved to France. Me, I wouldn't have come on my own.

In Tunisia we lived on the edge of our religion. My father was a commercial traveler, not at all strong on Jewish tradition. My grandfather was a native-born Algerian, which meant we were French nationals by birth —something that not all Tunisian Jews were privileged to be. But when Israel became a state in 1948, there was no great exodus of Jews from my country, as happened in Yemen, Iraq, Morocco. For someone without much education, I was doing very well in the police force. I was good at my job. If it was rare for a Jew to rise up in the ranks in Tunisia, it was even more rare in France. Yet in Paris I was almost certain to be promoted to commissioner.

And then suddenly one morning—it wasn't so long ago—Jean-Jacques said, "What is our country?" In France he had very few friends at school. He was dark like Tunisian Arabs, wore his hair long, and he felt different there. He kept hearing the expression *"sale Juif."* He was always asking me, "What is the difference between a French Catholic and a French Jew?" I told him the difference was unfortunate.

Our eldest daughter was the first to come to Israel. She sent for the next sister to join her. After a year or two, when they didn't come back, I began to wonder, Is it possible that they have done the right thing?

In 1971 I was in charge of a police district in Paris, near Bourget. I was named on the list for promotion to commissioner. I had just turned fifty, and I had twenty-five years of service, plus four years of war with the Free French. Appointment to the rank of police commissioner was virtually automatic. But when the list was published in June, I wasn't on it. I was the only one not promoted.

We had a family meeting about it, my wife, Jean-Jacques, and his two remaining sisters. By now a third sister had gone to Israel. "What do you think? What do you want to do?" Not one of them wanted to stay in France.

I left the police force July first, feeling that there was no country in the world where I could be at home.

We sailed in October. When we came in sight of Haifa, I gave Jean-Jacques the binoculars that had been a present from my colleagues in Paris. "When you get to Israel," they said, "you will be able to see the desert better." He looked. I looked. It seemed like a mirage, as if there were a halo over Haifa. I could see the port. When we got closer I could see people I knew—hundreds of Tunisians, my compatriots who had known me in Tunis as a young policeman—waiting to welcome us.

I found a job in Tel Aviv at the French Consulate. The consul was Catholic, but we knew each other from Tunis, where his house was alongside my mother's. The consul's son Thiery was the same age as Jean-Jacques, and they quickly became friends.

From the moment we arrived, Jean-Jacques felt at home. Everything about life in Israel exceeded his hopes and dreams.

He and his youngest sister went to a kibbutz to learn Hebrew. There was only a year between them. Jean-Jacques and Linda did everything together, on the kibbutz and then afterward at a special school here in Jaffa. Thiery, the consul's son, was also at the same school. The two boys were in the same class and they were to go to France together for a final year of school. Jean-Jacques had become interested in criminology. He wanted to be like me, a policeman. He was going to spend a year away before returning to do his army service and then continue his studies in criminology at the university.

He was to leave for Paris on a Saturday. Linda was to have gone with him but she had changed plans and decided to fly later. We had already bought his ticket, but on Friday the consul asked me if Jean-Jacques would mind waiting a day because on Sunday morning Thiery was also flying to Paris. "They can travel together," the consul said. It seemed like a good idea. So they left on Sunday morning.

The flight was scheduled to leave at nine, and we were very early. "Since it's only seven o'clock," the consul said, "why don't we try to get them on the air-bus that's leaving now?" There were two seats left on the air-bus so we exchanged the tickets and they left an hour earlier —on the flight heading for Athens that was hijacked to Entebbe, Uganda.

When we heard what had happened, we immediately sent a cable through the embassy to President Amin saying: WE THE PARENTS OF JEAN-JACQUES MIMOUNI AND

THIERY SICKER ARE PREPARED TO FLY TO UGANDA TO TAKE OUR CHILDREN'S PLACES AS HOSTAGES. What else could we do? We never got an answer to the cable.

At this stage the separation had not occurred. The boys were still together in the terminal building. I thought they would have stayed together from friendship. One was Jewish, one not, but they both had French passports and were born in the same town of Tunis.

From what I have heard, Jean-Jacques annoyed the German woman terrorist. It seems that she liked him, but at the same time she was annoyed because he was one of the hostages who organized games for the smaller children and put himself out running errands for the older people. "You're French," she said to him. "Why do you do this for the Jews?" "But I'm Jewish, too," he said. This is what the other passengers have told me.

When the hostages were divided, he went with the Jewish group. He stayed with the Israelis although his passport was French. Thiery went on to Paris when the French group was released. He is now back in Israel.

There are several versions of what happened when the Israeli troops arrived. Jean-Jacques was lying near the door. When the firing started, the German woman ran outside. She was shot but as she fell she threw a grenade which landed near the door where my son was lying. It fell beside his leg, but he didn't notice until a woman cried out to warn him. He jumped up. There was a bullet, then another and another. He was caught in the crossfire. I saw my son's body. His legs were scorched below where the grenade exploded as he jumped up. The man beside him was also killed and another man in the same

group was wounded. This man came to see me yesterday.

"Why my son? The only son? Why God, why mine?
Why from two hundred fifty people only mine?" I have
sworn that before dying I will avenge his death. But
how? Who will I kill? Those who are responsible, the
terrorists, are already dead. When the Israeli officer told
me the news, in the room at Lod airport, I hated him. I
hated Israel, Rabin, God, Golda Meir, the whole world.
I picked up a television set that was there and hurled it
at him across the room.

We didn't know. We thought he was alive. We were
woken at five in the morning with the news that the
rescue had succeeded and the hostages were coming
home. We were at Lod by seven. From seven until half
past ten we were drinking champagne. We were singing
and dancing. But I could see that my wife was uneasy.
I called a doctor, and he gave her some tablets to calm
her down. Then an announcement came over the loud-
speaker calling us to one side. Even then I still hoped.
But when you have been in the police as long as I have,
you know what an announcement like that means.

Linda left—she says she is finished with this country.
She went back to France. The consul also left. He felt
responsible and applied to be transferred. He went to
Canada. But the consul's son refused to leave, either for
France or Canada. He came to the house. "I have nothing
against him," I told my wife, "yet I cannot forgive him."
I wouldn't let him in.

The other day, on the anniversary of my son's death,

we gathered at the cemetery where my wife goes every day. His schoolmates came with their parents and teachers, the consul's son with them, hiding at the back. He didn't come forward. Yesterday he passed his final examinations. They would have finished together.

There was a time when if you had asked me, "What are you?" I would have answered "French." Why did I come to Israel? For me, it was a country out of history books, out of the Bible. It had no meaning. What am I? If you had asked that ten or even five years ago, I would have said without hesitation, *"Je suis Français."* Now I have a different feeling. I am still French at the consulate where I work, but I am French only inside. Outside the building I am Israeli.

My son knew who he was all the time. I found out only yesterday. When you live on the edge of your religion for so long and then discover what it is, you cannot put it aside any longer. Only a dog denies his breed.

The lawyers say we will get our hands on a lot of insurance money from this case. I will wait and see. Perhaps we could use the money to go somewhere to help my wife forget. But the money is meaningless. We could not live anywhere else now.

After living in Israel for five years you can ask to become a citizen. We have just done this. I don't believe that I can find peace outside this country where we have known great joy and great tragedy. And for Lola, it is the place she will never leave just because of this *malheur.* She says her place is here because our son is buried here.

13

Uzi Davidson

The minute they brought in the pack of passports, I knew it was going to happen. I didn't have to wait until the first name was called. And I told Sarah and the boys that when we are called, we'll go.

They called out the names from the passports—they had had two days to sort them and it wasn't too difficult. An Israeli passport is not so obscure. They called a few other names as well, including an American couple who protested—they had every right to protest, because they didn't have Israeli passports—and the Mimouni boy, who was on a French passport.

I wouldn't say that it didn't shake me. It did. There was a selection. But they called my name and I went. You don't have a choice.

When Sarah and I were younger, when we were engaged, the question we asked ourselves was, why did none of the six million Jews ever do anything when they were selected? At Entebbe I found out why. You never believe you are going to die.

Not even for one moment of that hell did I believe I was going to die.

I wasn't the only trained soldier among the passengers. There were others. On the second or third day I remember taking a head count, and we discussed the possibility of overpowering the terrorists. We dropped it almost immediately because of where we were. We were not threatened, only by Idi Amin. And he doesn't count.

The Ugandans brought mattresses—carloads of new mattresses and blankets and towels, brand new. Towels that you couldn't use because they hadn't been soaked, they were stiff. Big Daddy Amin's contribution.

They kept the lights on in the terminal. The first night was bad, but after that I didn't have difficulty sleeping. The human being is an animal that accommodates itself like an animal. I slept very well. I never discussed the separation—the selection—with the boys; they wouldn't have understood. Ron was sixteen, Benny thirteen. The only thing I said was that we shouldn't be afraid for our lives. I said it all the time, continuously, because I remembered past experiences like Ma'alot. I'm a realistic level-headed sabra, also a pilot, a navigator. Since it was clear to me there was no military solution to Entebbe—we didn't have a plane that could fly that far from Israel—I thought there would be negotiations, some exchange made to free us like in Algiers. I never felt alone there, not for a single minute. This way, that way, the other way—I was convinced the government of Israel would *not* leave us alone. It's a very big thing to feel, believe me. And I'm speaking now from experience.

The Israeli task force came a few minutes too soon. Sarah and Ron were playing bridge, Benny was lying half asleep, and I was reading a book called *The Eagle Has*

Landed, about a German raid on England to kidnap Churchill. I didn't finish the book. The task force arrived when I was on the last two pages. Ron was left with eight cards in his hand. He must have tucked them away as we dived down. He found them later in his back pocket.

I was afraid that if they started shooting at random, a lot of people would be hurt. I grabbed my family, and we dived down and ran very fast toward the corridor. The firing continued and it looked a little strange. A *little* strange? It looked *very* strange. My mind was a blank. The only thing I knew was we would *keep on lying down* with our heads low *until it gets quiet.* And then we'd see. Then somebody said, "There's an Israeli soldier." I lifted my head and I saw him. From that moment on it was the most normal, the most natural thing that should happen. There was no elation, no how or why or which way. They were there, and we were going home.

Entebbe made no difference to my attitude about living here. Maybe for some, like my brother who went to America thirty years ago, there is a choice. I'm an Israeli, a Jew, and that's it. For me there's a choice without a choice. Or, I can phrase it another way: I choose to think that I have no choice.

But if you ask me whether or not Entebbe adds a point to the literature of anti-Semitism, it does. They looked for the Jews.

There are some Jews who are masochists. I don't think we are the type. I don't believe that I have any sense of persecution, either openly or subconsciously, and I don't believe that Israel as a state has any. But with the same clear mind I would say that history proves certain things about us. For some reason—I don't know why—we are chosen. You might say discriminated against. I'm not boasting, I'm stating it as a fact. And if it is so, if there is any connection between this discrimination and this land, then the only reason to live here is in order to make it a fact—to consummate it.

My mother's mother was born in Jerusalem, and we have a history in Jerusalem for I don't know how many generations. I've never bothered to research into my roots. My father's parents came from Russia-Poland in the 1890s and settled in Rishon Le-Zion, the first Jewish settlement here, founded in 1882. Father and Mother were born in Rishon, they grew up in Rishon, they married in Rishon, they raised their children in Rishon, and to this day they live there. I don't know what Israel was for my father's people, a place to live maybe. I never thought to ask.

The Israeli government has just released forty terrorists in exchange for the return of eleven soldiers killed in the last war. Forty live terrorists in exchange for eleven bodies. This is important—it's important for the family to feel that its kin is being brought to burial properly. I believe you have to honor the memory. And if they want live terrorists for that, I don't think it matters if we have a few more or a few less in our prisons. But this is a very different thing from releasing terrorists for hostages, which is a form of submission we cannot allow ourselves —unless there is no other choice.

If there is a choice, if we can do something, we should never release terrorists, even though as happened in Ma'alot children were killed when the soldiers went in. A terrible result, but still a good result in my opinion. This is one of the things we have to bear. Because this is a war, it's a continuous war. When there's a war, people die.

It's the government's right to demand my life; only, having asked for my life, they have to defend it.

Israel is now being argued into a corner. Israel will always be argued into a corner. We're small and we're weak—a small country is a weak country by definition. We're poor in natural resources. We have all the good reasons to be argued into corners. We have to go into negotiations and fight. In my opinion we shouldn't give anything back, *anything,* but maybe we will be forced to do it. When we are forced, we will do it.

I don't believe that 1973 was the last war. Peace in our time is not something I believe in. You live here and there's an awareness of danger—as kids we went to school in armored buses. The inauguration of the state of Israel was on Friday, May 15. Early Saturday morning Tel Aviv was bombed. The planes passed very low over our house. At one point Rishon was bombed. These are facts of life and you live with it, just as in Jerusalem today if you go into any Jewish institution, you are searched. If you walk into an Arab institution or a Christian institution, nobody bothers. So every day you are reminded: The war is on, but only against the Jews. I'm aware of this, yet I don't think it affects the way I am or how I think.

Take my brother in America. When something

happens here, some outbreak, he's more worried than I am. The difference has to do with involvement, with being close to the scene and knowing what's really happening.

Like I said, I choose to believe that I have no choice. Don't let me repeat what I said before. You have to have something to belong to, a family, a heritage. The place for a Jew should be Israel, but the place for an Israeli, it *is.*

Maybe I could live in America. I speak English. Both Sarah and I have a command of languages, we've traveled. Now the question would not be Why *not* live in America?, but *Why* live in America? Give me a good reason. I could probably earn a better living there. Is that enough reason? I don't say I haven't ever considered it, but when I did, the whole point seemed to be to make a lot of money and then come back and live here better than I do now. I live well enough as I am.

My brother came here once with his wife just before the Six Day War and tried to settle, but it didn't work out. I was angry when he decided to go back to the States. I criticized him very hotly because I believed he was hurting the family, especially my father. My father is a family man. It hurt him, for instance, that I left Rishon to live in Tel Aviv. So when my brother went to live in the States, it was much worse.

I don't criticize my brother anymore—it's not a tragedy if somebody leaves. But it is considered some sort of betrayal. It's interesting. We call the immigrants who come to Israel *olim,* the Hebrew word for "ascending." Those who leave are called *yordim,* the word for "descending."

I didn't tell you, but after we got back from Entebbe we turned straight round and went to the States, which is where we were going when we started out, before we were hijacked. We came back Saturday. Sunday morning I went to the Foreign Office to get a new passport. The clerk didn't understand what I wanted. I said, "Look, I came back yesterday. My plan is to go almost immediately, and I'd appreciate it if you would prepare our passports as soon as possible. I don't know if you know, but our passports were left at Entebbe."

"So what do you need a new passport for?"

I said, "I'm going away, I'm leaving."

He said, "Are you crazy?"

14

Pastor Bob Lindsay

After I succeed in getting through to all these obtuse Jews, give me another thousand years and I'll make them missionaries to the world. That's what they ought to be doing instead of all this in-gathering and feeling that the Christian world, the Gentile world, is against them. Although historically speaking they're correct, biblically speaking it's an illusion, sheer illusion.

A lot of Jewish suffering has been caused by Christians. So where does this leave me, a Christian, preaching the Gospel in Jerusalem? It means I've got two or three strikes against me before I start—but that isn't the real problem. The real problem is that no Jew knows how he can be a Christian and a Jew at the same time.

I remember one time I took an American man and his wife to a Jewish colony in the north. We had a young Israeli as our guide. The woman was a very keen Christian and she began to testify about Jesus. The guide took me aside and said, "They're Gentile, aren't they? What can a goy understand about us?" He assumed I was Jewish of course.

This is a problem of identity the Jews have been trying to solve for hundreds of years. The very success of this state doesn't solve it.

Tell a Jew that here is another Jew, an Orthodox Jew who comes to my church and preaches, who believes in Jesus Christ, and he says "impossible." Tell an Israeli, "Well, all Christians are really Jewish," and you cut the ground from under his feet. He immediately thinks, "What's the point of my being different from anybody else?" This frightens him to tears because he has been *saved* from religion by becoming Israeli. He has accepted a definition of the term *Jew* which is automatically not Christian.

Brother, I don't know what the answer is or when they will get over their persecution complex, but I know what the stumbling block is, where the crucial departure lies —*Jesus.* Jesus just happens to be the biggest Jew that ever lived. And if he's as big as I and my Orthodox Jewish friend think he is, that's more important than all the things false Christians did to Jews through the years or false Jews did to Christians in earlier periods.

There's this basic dichotomy: "We Jews, and all the Gentiles." This is part of the Jewish mentality. The Israeli may be ever so nonreligious but he is still somehow bound to this concept. Of course it has to do with his instinct for survival—but as a Jew.

I grew up in Oklahoma, and I preached to very poor people—renters and sharecroppers, characters out of *The Grapes of Wrath.* How many Jews did I know? I knew Mr. Tannenbaum in his pawnshop. In other words, not very many.

But in college I began to meet young Jews. I asked

myself, "If the Gospel is for everyone—and it certainly was for the Jews in the First Century—why isn't there some Christian who lives and works among the Jewish people now?" Then, in the Book of Matthew, I came across the following verse, "Go not into any way of the Gentiles nor into any city of the Samaritans but go rather to the lost sheep of the House of Israel." That verse became the turning point in my life. In early 1939 I came to Israel with a Bible study group. We were one of the first big tours allowed in after the riots ended. Everyone else in the group went back, but I stayed and learned Hebrew, wandered about Trans-Jordan, and lived with Jews and Arabs. I had an accordion I played for various mission groups, but it was the language that fascinated me. I knew Greek, I'd majored in classical Greek for the New Testament. But I needed Hebrew for the Old Testament.

It took me a long time to understand what it means to be part of a minority like the Jewish people. Like a man trying to understand a woman, it's the opposite of what you know.

When you talk to Jews today you realize that the average Jewish person thinks of himself as part of a religion unrelated to Christianity. "All Christians are Gentiles, we Jews are God's people." That's his mythology. The average Christian person has ambivalent feelings about Jews. "Jews are good because Jesus was Jewish. And Peter and John. . . ." He associates the terms *Jews* with the people in the Bible but at the same time he supposes that the Jews killed Christ—there's that other side of the coin he's thinking of all the time. "We Christians are not Jews." That's his mythology. So we have a double mythology. What it is of course is a semantic break, dating from postbiblical Jewish history. Very few people know much about it, except Jews.

In the New Testament all Christians were Jews. In North Africa, for instance, Jews and Christians were buried in the same cemeteries. As late as the fourth century you find St. Augustine writing to the Christians in North Africa: "Don't call yourselves Jews anymore." In other words, for two or three hundred years after Christ died the relationship between Christians and Jews was very keen. Christians were a Jewish sect.

Living here I thought of myself as Jewish. As Paul says, "We're children of Abraham by faith." In effect I began saying, "I am not a goy." I said it many times. I say it all the time in my church.

Paul says it. "*When* you were Gentile . . . ," he tells the people of Corinth. For *Gentile* read *pagan*. When Paul converted the pagans of Corinth, he gave them a Jewish inheritance—the history of Abraham and Isaac down to Jesus and the Apostles. Until then these pagans *had no history*. Now, in becoming Jewish Christians, they gained a double history. They entered the Jewish family stream.

In other words, I see it this way. You have a stream moving, an earthly stream. Whole civilizations move into it and come to a vertical harmonious position with God. You ultimately have a church, a believing body. Christendom eventually becomes a reality, and so there is a whole historical thing I call Judeo-Christendom— "an earthly people of God," if you want to call it that. Paul calls them "the Beloved," the people God has concern with in history.

I deny that there is a Jewish stream that is meaningful —ultimately meaningful—outside the Jewish-Christendom stream. I say I still feel Jewish.

How do I describe myself? I'm a pastor preaching in Jerusalem who feels himself to be Jewish, but I'm not a Jewish pastor. I'm a Jewish *Christian* pastor. I don't think there is any other kind of Christian.

Christianity *is* Jewish. There is no *exit* from this.

Christians don't understand it either.

I preach here without restrictions. I've been here for so long I feel an insider. But I'm still critical. I have to be critical, I have to say, "Yes, it's a fine sort of thing, Zionism, as far as it goes." I'm all for saving the Jewish people. Good gracious, who wants anybody to die? As long as you are saying that Israel is a place of refuge for the Jewish people, anybody with an ounce of common sense will say, "right." But when you now define the term *Jew* and don't include *me* . . . !

I want to be able to come to this country and say, "I am a Jew and therefore I have a right to return to this land under the Law of Return like every other Jew." But here they only think of a Jewish person as having been born of a Jewish mother or of not having adopted another religion. There's a deadlock. It's true that Jewish people think in historical parallels, of what's been done to them through the years. But they also *don't* think this way. The young Israelis think their fathers were carrots because they didn't fight; these kids don't think about Germany and anti-Semitism the way their parents did. This is a hopeful thing, an evolutionary thing—a result of what I would call "normalization": people living like any other people without being afraid, accepting differences and not fearing that they have to think a certain way in order to remain Jewish because the law says so. It's a hopeful sign.

I wanted to live amongst Jews and I'm doing it. What's more, I feel Israeli. I may not have taken out Israeli citizenship, but they don't know I'm not an Israeli—that's why I can be critical. I have an Israeli mentality, and you won't find an Israeli who is not critical. I am so related to these people. I know all their jokes. The most Israeli thing about me is that I speak Hebrew. That's important. I belong as much as the next fellow, even if I didn't take part in their wars. I was here in '48. I was here during the siege.

When it got rough—barricades were set up, people were shooting back and forth—this house became a kind of asylum. We had fifteen, sixteen Jewish refugees living here besides ourselves. Arabs moved out of Jewish areas and Jews left Arab areas. There was an exchange of populations. We set up a kitchen and a little hostel. Then things got so bad that I sent my wife and children home to Oklahoma because I saw that Jerusalem was going to be under siege. But we managed to keep services going during the siege.

I was left in charge here. It was a difficult time. Things were breaking up. It was my war, too. We were very much identified with it, although we were not doing any fighting. I suppose if they had asked me to take up a gun and defend this area I might have done so. But they didn't.

When the Old City fell in '48 I don't think I felt the

loss personally—I didn't feel it was mine to lose. Nor did I think it was the Jews' to lose.

I think my main concern is being a citizen of Heaven. So it's not *that* important to me to be in Jerusalem, although I feel at home here. It's just that I'm better prepared to serve the Lord here. If I died tomorrow, what would I have accomplished? I don't know. I hope I would get to Heaven and talk to the Lord about it.

What is important for me is the people and the people that I'm working with. Yesterday we had a service with perhaps twelve or fifteen Jewish people participating. Tomorrow we will have a baptism. The two people who have asked for the baptism are both Jewish people. That's who I'm dealing with. Earlier I went to visit a neighbor who had had a prostate operation. Before he went to the hospital I said that we'd be glad to pray for him. At first he objected, but when he went to the hospital he said, "Pray for me." And when he got back he said, "I saw your prayer."

What else can I say? You remember the cliché, "Aw, some of my best friends are Jews." I'd probably have to say, "All of my best friends are Jews."

There's a fellow right now, a government official, who's been coming to services. The other night he said he had decided that he had no other option than to believe that Jesus was the Messiah. If he should ever ask me, I'd baptize him. His friends will call him a renegade, some will look at him askance, but that's what Jesus does, you know. If there is truth, truth always separates people.

The Israeli thinks of himself as separate. Well, as I said at the start, it's an illusion. There's justification but it's still an illusion if you think biblically. You heard about the Northern soldier who came to a Southern town just after the American Civil War? A black lady waited on him. She came ambling up and he said, "Why so slow? Don't you know you're *free*?" She looked at him. "Yeah, Lincoln's freed the slaves," he said. "You're free." Total surprise to her. She got very happy when she finally understood what had happened. But she was a slave until that moment, in her mind.

All I'm saying is that both Christians and Jews are totally wrong in their understanding of their semantic relations.

Take Entebbe: Israeli people to the right, all others to the left. Where do I belong?

I actually belong with the people in the Jewish group. But they won't understand that. Nor would the other people at Entebbe understand it.

15

Abba Kovner

During the trial of Adolph Eichmann, in one part of my testimony I tried to make clear that special feeling of isolation common to European Jews. In answer to a question from one of the judges, I explained that there were three walls of isolation. The first wall was a physical wall that the Germans put up between us and the world. If you tore down this wall there was another one—the neighbors you lived with before the war, who had become themselves a threatening wall. And then behind this there was a third wall—a feeling that the whole world outside was indifferent.

I had been hiding in a convent in the hills and I came down to the ghetto in December, at Christmas. I was not the only one in hiding. There were other boys like me and some girls who were hiding in another convent. Until then we had been patient, like the people in the ghetto.

My father advised patience. A Jew, he said, has to bend down in order to remain erect. After that you can stand up and be proud. It was the central point of my education.

I lived in Vilna, symbol of the dispersion—"Little Jerusalem of the Diaspora." As a child I saw myself in Israel—I was a dreamer—so when I was eleven I made a flying machine from a bicycle and jumped out of a high window. When I discovered I could not fly to Israel I built myself a small boat, a canoe. Our house was beside a stream and I thought I could sail to the Baltic and reach the Promised Land that way. I actually set out. I almost drowned. I belong to those people, no doubt there are many of us, who echo the words of Agnon when he received the Nobel Prize: "I was born in Jerusalem, but because of a historical accident I was two thousand years out." In fact, except for another accident of history, I might have been born there, because in 1917 my parents set out for Israel, but when they got to Sebastopol they were caught by the Revolution. My father ran out of money and I was born in Sebastopol in the middle of the civil war. My father was taken prisoner, first by the counterrevolutionaries and then by the revolutionaries. Things went from bad to worse, and we started wandering from place to place. Eventually we returned to Vilna.

At twelve I made a vow. My father was a cantor and I wanted to have a fine voice like his, so one day I stood up and sang out strongly. Everyone laughed, but I defended myself, saying, "I'm composing, I'm not out of tune. The music is original." Then I wrote down my vow: "If God will grant me a good voice"—because Mother had said that my voice would soon change—"I will give ten years of my life to the Holy One, blessed be He." I believed then in all innocence in the existence of God.

We were eleven boys hidden in a small Catholic convent outside the town. We were dressed as nuns, isolated from the town. It was dangerous for the sisters. Later, after we went down to the ghetto, the mother superior came and smuggled arms and explosives to us. There was also a German officer who helped us with transport. Sometimes the girls from the other convent, also disguised as nuns, came and told us what was going on.

For me the war had begun in 1941 when the Germans built the ghetto in Vilna. Jews had been killed before the ghetto was built but not systematically. People were disoriented. They hid under tables and in cupboards, but they were found. We, the young people of our movement (I was twenty-three, the oldest), found hiding places for others, but we knew nothing about weapons. We had taken vows against any form of militarism.

Between June and September and then again in December there were big *aktions,* or roundups. I visited the ghetto during one of these *aktions* and watched. Like everyone else, I didn't know where they were taking these people. But when I went back to the convent I began to think about what I had seen. I also questioned people who came to the convent from outside.

There was a priest who came to say mass for the nuns. Afterward I took him onto a hill, and for the first time he told me about Ponar. He spoke in a shadowy fashion and I felt he was hiding something. But he told me that Jews were being taken to Ponar in carts, and the carts were coming back empty. I began to build up a picture.

The Germans said the ghetto was overcrowded and that they were taking people to another ghetto where there was a labor camp and factories. In one ghetto would be those who could work and in the other those who weren't fit to work. The people believed this. But with my eyes I had seen that there was no logic to the selection. For example, the Germans said they were taking out the "unskilled," but some of those they took were highly skilled and many who were left had no skills at all. In other words, it was a lie. So the priest's story about Ponar began to arouse questions in me. The problem was to ask the questions.

The first question I asked myself was, Is this a spontaneous pogrom? I realized that a large part of the Jewish population of Vilna was no longer there. Forty thousand Jews had disappeared within six months.

The second question: If there *is* another ghetto, why haven't we had word from it? There is no isolation possible without a rumor. The conclusion must be that the other ghetto is not there. In other words, the people who were taken no longer exist.

I asked myself another question: Is this the act of a local German commander? And I decided that it couldn't be—no local commander has such power. It must be a system.

Then I came to the worst conclusion of all—and the hardest—because up to this point some people were ready to agree with me. But on this last point, nobody. I wrote in my manifesto that this was a systematic extermination of the Jews in Europe, and we Jews in Vilna are only the first in the queue. I remember the moment I reached this conclusion. I was *absolutely certain*.

There was no escape, because there was nowhere left to escape to. Nobody wanted to believe it, not even the Judenrat, the ghetto authorities, although they knew.

They knew about Ponar. They knew because Sara had come. Sara was nineteen. She had escaped from Ponar and crawled twenty miles back to Vilna. But the Jewish authorities didn't want her to talk, because they knew there would be panic. So they hid Sara. I found her and she told me her story. How the Germans put the people in a line and shot them, first a hundred and then another hundred and another. How she was wounded and fell into the pit on top of the dead. How she crawled out of the pit. How from afar she heard more shooting. And there were no houses there, no dwellings, no factories. No ghetto, only a pit in the forest, a place for shooting.

There were other survivors, Sara wasn't the only one. The evidence mounted up. My manifesto was a call to arms, a leaflet we distributed in the ghetto. The discussions were bitter. After January 1942, there was a lull without any roundups, a stabilizing period of about a year. Most people in the ghetto thought the tragedy was over.

Fighting, armed resistance, what did it mean? It meant immediate personal danger. Not only that, but everything that we did—like getting hold of weapons or acts of sabotage—endangered everyone. Vitka, my wife, was the first woman in Europe to destroy a German military train. We could have gathered weapons and saved ourselves by escaping to the forests, but we made the opposite decision. We brought all our people from outside the ghetto and we moved into the ghetto. Spiritually we did it for them, but in fact it caused conflict. At one point there was nearly civil war in the ghetto. They had hope, and we destroyed the hope.

The greatest dilemma was when friends arrived from

Warsaw and told of a reality there that was completely different. There was no killing there. Was I wrong? I began to have doubts, but I didn't change my opinion. And to my sorrow I was right.

I believed that sooner or later the others would see it correctly. I didn't say that fighting would save us—nobody believed that, I didn't believe it myself. Look, even I had no solution. I only said that if I have to die I will choose the way. I will decide my fate for myself. Afterward, we realized that by fighting you can save even yourself. In a situation where there is no hope, fighting creates a sort of hope.

My mother and brothers were in the ghetto (my father had died), but I didn't live with them. They knew nothing of what I was doing. This was another loneliness, this separation from your own kind. To get arms we stole. I am ashamed to say we stole money from our fellow Jews, and with the money we bought weapons on the black market. We used the sewers. We read books on chemistry and manufactured mines. The first time the mother superior of St. Catherine's came she brought me two grenades. I had never seen a grenade.

Organizing a resistance, it's not public relations. We began with twenty, then thirty, forty. People came over to us gradually, in twos and threes. In the end we were two hundred fifty fighters.

Most of the people didn't know of our existence. Not even the Judenrat knew, until we told them. The problem of building a resistance in the ghetto was how to hide it and at the same time exist, because it was a conspiracy. The ghetto was so small—how can I tell you? There were five little streets, each with ten houses. I speak of five streets and twenty thousand people.

Why didn't the others see it correctly? Why did they go to their deaths *kacha,* meekly, like that? In all persecutions before Hitler there was always the possibility that a Jew could remain alive. Either he could turn Christian or he could leave. It happened in Spain, so he went to Italy; it happened in Italy, so he went to Germany. He could escape from one town to another. If the persecution was because of property, he could give up his property. But now, even if he became a Christian it didn't help, because the Nuremberg laws went back three generations. Jews who were no longer Jews were still put into the ghetto. And giving up your property didn't help because it had already been taken away. In all the long history of persecution this was the first time that a state, an imperial power, had decided to annihilate the Jews biologically. As a program of state.

The *totality* of the annihilation—this was the change. The totality, and the absence of spontaneity. The result was a psychological situation unprecedented in history. The ghetto was a place designed for annihilation. On the wall of the ghetto the Germans wrote HIER IST TYPHUS, so that people wouldn't enter. In the eyes of the German population the people inside were reduced to vermin, to nonpeople.

It is against this background that you must understand the passive acceptance and the passive resistance. If the Jews of Vilna could preserve their sanity, could stay clean and free of infection, could educate their children —because it was forbidden to send the children to schools—could distribute what little food there was, if they could do all this against the background of dehumanization, it was already significant. It was already a form of resistance.

Afterward, the few people who came out to join us in the forests did stay alive. We escaped through the sewers. I went out with the last group at the last moment. Vitka was with me, also a brother of mine who joined the partisans and was later killed. He was killed not by the Germans but by the partisans—they took away his weapon. Because in the forests there was also anti-Semitism.

We were a Jewish partisan group and at first we were the only one. Then came the Russian, the Lithuanian, the Ukrainian partisans. We were very close to one another in the forest. They were better armed than we were. They had two or three guns each, we had almost nothing. They gave us nothing. They hid the weapons. If they could, they disarmed us. It is a story common to every forest. There were many hundreds of Jewish partisans, but the world does not know because we were swallowed by the Russians, the Poles, the Ukrainians, the Byelorussians, the Czechs, the Yugoslavs. It is very simple—they did not want us. We had to fight to stay together as a group. This was another kind of isolation.

My brother and his group were killed in this way. They came from the ghetto to the forest with weapons. In the forest the Russian partisans took away their weapons. The Germans attacked, and all thirty of them were killed. We were all fighting the same enemy, but we were fighting two wars: one war against the Germans and another against the other partisans.

After the war, the isolation did not go away. Despite the fact that we had a few non-Jewish friends who wanted to help us, they were so few, such an insignificant minority, it didn't change the overriding feeling of total isolation. I am still haunted by it.

The mother superior who brought us arms was taken by the Gestapo. The little sisters of the convent who sheltered us were taken. The German officer who gave us transport did not survive.

It is not only that we were isolated as Jews. Intellectually I realized that it is the tragedy of the weak, that in a critical situation the weak are abandoned. And the lesson of this experience is the recognition of two opposing elements. One is that the show of power—Jewish power—is a condition for survival. But power is not the answer to everything. There is also ethos and spirit. These two elements live together in me, and conflict—and not only in me. You can see it in Israel.

When I first arrived in Israel and saw a cypress tree, I laughed. I remembered reading the first Hebrew novel written in Lithuania a century ago in which the hero meets a lion on the banks of the Jordan. He escapes by climbing to the top of a cypress tree and he sits there. When I saw how pointed a cypress is I realized that it was impossible to sit up there. As a child I was fed stories and lullabies, and to me this land was both a reality and a dream, so much so that I even knew the landscape. Seeing that cypress tree, I finally understood the difference between the dream and the reality.

I always thought that with the creation of Israel anti-

Semitism would die. That was also a mistake of our dream. When I was in America recently there was a book published called *The Greatest Hoax of the Century* which denies that six million Jews perished in Europe. It is part of the new wave of propaganda. This is symptomatic. I am pessimistic, but not resigned. What was it that engulfed us? What was the borderline of the Holocaust? It wasn't fear but helplessness, a collective helplessness. Israel is an end to the helplessness.

For me it's like the shirt hanging on the hanger. The shirt is the Jewish people and the hanger is Israel. If the hanger falls, the shirt will fall. And the hanger without the shirt has no meaning.

Today we have anti-Semitism in the form of Arab attacks. Anti-Israel is the new cloth of anti-Semitism. If once anti-Semitism was directed against the Jew as a Jew or the Jew as a community, today it is directed against Israel as a state. Maybe we are an index to the genuine basic processes in the history of mankind. The psychological walls that surround us have not changed; they appear only in a different form. I don't know how many walls there are today, I only know that the people of my generation no longer have a sense of helplessness. I prefer to see not the walls themselves but the gaps between the walls through which it is possible to have ties and friends.

Today I read in the paper that Mt. Etna is spouting lava for a distance of two miles. The volcanologists say that this is quite normal, that it is only when it reaches the critical point of three miles that it becomes dangerous. If this is so in nature, this is how it is in our history among nations. We plant trees, we build homes, we sow gardens, but on the horizon there is always a volcano that will not go away.

It is a long story. For me Israel and the Jewish people have become fused in terms of survival. Here now it is the same symphony, with variations. There are those who play the symphony in C minor and those who play it in B minor, but the fact is that this is the only place where the remnant of the Jewish people can hope for a renaissance without fear of annihilation.

How long did it take me to get here? A hundred years.

Postscript

It is a rare thing to enter the home of fifteen strangers in a strange land and make fifteen friends, but because of this book I know it is possible. I thank these people for their welcome, for their trust, and for expanding my education. Any credit for these pages is theirs as much as mine.

Three episodes call for comment.

Sylva Zalmanson (Chapter 4) has now been joined in Israel by her brother, Izrail (released in 1978), and her husband and another brother, Wulf, both released in 1979 as this book went to press. Her third brother, Samuel, is still imprisoned in the Soviet Union. For a further view of the Leningrad hijack trials, see Edward Kuznetsov's *Prison Diaries* (Vallentine, Mitchell, 1975), which were written secretly and smuggled out to the West.

Ada Sereni (Chapter 5) was known in Italy as "the woman in black" and at various secret rendezvous became a symbol of hope to tens of thousands of refugees awaiting transport to Palestine between 1945 and 1948. Ada's own account of the venture lay in a drawer unpublished for twenty years. It appeared finally in Milan as *I Clandestini del Mare* ("Ships Without Flags," Mursia, 1973). Ruth Bondy has written a full and fine account of the life of Enzo Sereni: *The Emissary* (Little, Brown, 1977).

In 1954 a memorial service for the parachutists from Palestine who died fulfilling their missions, including Enzo Sereni, was held by the Sea of Galilee. During the ceremony a small plane bringing a message from the President crashed out of control among the spectators. Among those killed were Ada and Enzo's only son Daniel and his wife.

Abba Kovner's manifesto (Chapter 15), issued from the Vilna ghetto in December 1941, was the first public proclamation that the Jews of Europe were being sent to their destruction as part of a system of mass biological extermination. His manifesto ("Ponar is not a labor camp. All of them are shot . . .") came six months before the Warsaw rising and raised the alarm.

After the war Abba Kovner worked in the underground in Europe, reached Palestine illegally, and settled on a kibbutz near Tel Aviv where he still lives. Sometimes called "the poet of the Resistance," he has been awarded the Israeli Prize for Literature. His verse, translated from the Hebrew by Shirley Kaufman, has appeared in America and England. He is responsible for creating Beth Hatefutsoth, the new Diaspora museum, which opened in Tel Aviv in 1978.

Acknowledgments

In the course of preparing this book I made inordinate demands on many people who do not appear in the text, and I acknowledge their help, of many kinds, with a deep gratitude. Their names appear below:

Hilde Alexander-Katz, Kalman Bar'On, Ruth Bar'On, Violet Battat, Alexander Berlyne, Shoshana Blum, Jack Campbell, Dr. Gad and Chava Chadar, Michael Elkins, Menachem and Vera Eyal, Rabbi Jacob Goldman, Yosef Hassin, Rosa Israel, Benjamin Jaffe, Zev Kedem, Victor and Suzi Levi, Sarah and Josef Menachem, George Ney, Yair and Irit Palmoni, Moshe Pearlman, Ari Rath, Adele Rothman, Professor Aharon and Yoheved Shulov, Eric Silver, David and Dahlia Sommer, Moshe Yegar; also Fay Doron and Yoel Palgi, both of whom died before the manuscript was completed.

I am indebted to Ruth Bondy for kindly reading the manuscript before publication and to the following people for their help with interpreting and translating: Hannah Amit-Kochavi, Edna Berlyne, Gila Brand, Itta Horol, Vitka Kempner, Pierre Motyl, Shulamit Serkatz, Michael Shashar, Miriam Shiloh, and Baruch Sugarman.

In a land where everyone has three jobs, they gave up time freely and, in cases, everything short of defense commitments to overcome my linguistic ineptitude. I owe a debt to Christine Sewell, of Hamilton, New Zealand, for typing the first draft, to Baruch Ginzberg, of Tel Aviv, typewriter mechanic and savior, to Ted Braaten of New York, for all the double quotation marks, and to my editor, Bobbi Mark, for her great care and patience. To my wife Helen, who not only researched the book with me and found subjects I might have ignored, but also solved many puzzles through the various drafts, my loving gratitude.

Glossary

Aliya: The great immigration.
Bar mitzvah: ("Man of duty") Ceremony performed at 13 when a Jewish boy takes on the responsibility of adulthood.
Gush Emunim: A very religious person.
Haganah: Illegal Jewish army during the time of the British mandate.
Kipah: Cap worn by orthodox Jews.
Kolchoz: Collective farm in Soviet Union.
Mitzvah: A good deed.
Moshav, moshav shitufi: Types of Israeli cooperative village.
Mukhtar: Head man in Arab village.
Oleh chadash: A new immigrant.
Palmach: Youth corps of shock troops, forerunner of today's commandos.
Sabra: Native-born Israeli.
Shaliach (pl. shlihim): Emissary.
Shiksah: Non-Jewish girl.
Shuk: Arab market.
Shul: Synagogue.
Talis: Prayer shawl.